TRESWELL'S SURVEY OF PURBECK

RALPH TRESWELL'S SURVEY
OF SIR CHRISTOPHER HATTON'S LANDS
IN PURBECK, 1585 – 6

Edited by

MARK FORREST

With contributions by

JENNY HALLING BARNARD

ROSE MITCHELL

MARTIN PAPWORTH

DORSET RECORD SOCIETY

VOLUME 19

Published 2017 by Dorset Record Society
Dorset History Centre, Bridport Road, Dorchester, Dorset DT1 1RP

in association with the National Trust

Typeset in ITC New Baskerville by John Chandler,
and printed by Lightning Source

British Library Cataloguing in Publication Data:
A catalogue record for this book is available from the British Library.

ISBN 978-0-900339-22-6

CONTENTS

ACKNOWLEDGEMENTS

IN COMPLETING THIS volume Dorset Record Society pays tribute to all those who have supported the project. It is most grateful to the National Trust and the Dorset History Centre for permission to publish this edition of Ralph Treswell's survey of Sir Christophher Hatton's lands and rights in Purbeck (reference D/BKL/E/A/3/1).

We would also like to thank The National Archives and Northamptonshire Record Office for permission to reproduce images from their collections, and the Environment Agency for permission to reproduce the LiDAR survey of Studland.

Many people have assisted in preparing this edition, in particular: John and Sue Rowntree and Louise Haywood have generously supplied information from their own research projects. Ann Smith, Brannah Mackenzie, Antony Wilsdon and Graham Hoddinott have been of great assistance in reading and commenting on sections of the text.

Special thanks are due to John Chandler for his advice and work on the production, layout and typesetting of the volume.

The National Trust and National Lottery players through funding from the Heritage Lottery Fund (HLF) have made this publication possible.

THE CONTRIBUTORS

 After completing an MSc in Care of Collections at Cardiff University, **Jenny Halling Barnard** worked for the National Trust at their South Somerset properties. She then attended West Dean College, Chichester, graduating with a GDip and PGDip in the Conservation of Books and Library Materials. After completing an Institute of Conservation internship at the North Yorkshire County Record Office she became Conservator at Durham County Record Office. Jenny moved to Dorset to take up position as Archive Conservator at Dorset History Centre in 2015. She has written articles for peer publications and has presented a paper on the use of volunteers in conservation projects at the Archives and Record Association Conference.

 **Mark Forrest** is an archivist at the Dorset History Centre where he manages the paper and parchment collections. He completed a PhD on the estates of Chertsey Abbey and worked for Cambridge and London Universities, editing and indexing medieval and early modern documents, before moving to Dorset in 2004. Mark has published on a range of social and economic subjects including the uses of manorial documents, the Black Death in Dorset, women holding public office in late medieval England, tax distribution in the fifteenth century and changes to the fifteenth century economy in the southwest. He is Dorset editor for *Somerset and Dorset Notes and Queries*

 **Rose Mitchell** is map specialist at The National Archives. She co-authored *Maps: their untold stories: map treasures from The National Archives* (Bloomsbury, 2014), with Andrew Janes, and *Maps for family and local history* (Public Record Office, 2003) with Geraldine Beech. She has written and spoken on the use of maps in various forms of historical research, including military and colonial maps, sea charts, and architectural drawings. Her specialism is sixteenth-century maps, including maps by Ralph Treswell senior and junior in The National Archives. She is a fellow of the Royal Geographical Society and grew up in West Dorset.

 **Martin Papworth** studied archaeology, local history and landscape studies at Weymouth College and Bristol University and has worked as an archaeologist for the National Trust since 1986. He advises on the conservation of sites and monuments in Dorset, Somerset, Wiltshire and Gloucestershire within their South West Region. His first job for the National Trust was to carry out archaeological and historic landscape surveys across the newly acquired Corfe Castle and Kingston Lacy Estates, enabling him to become well acquainted with the extraordinary range of documents within the Bankes family archive. Martin has published various research articles on National Trust properties in Dorset including Corfe Castle, medieval Kingston Lacy and the Iron Age and Roman settlements in and around Badbury Rings. His PhD examined the Late Iron Age communities of the Dorset environs, published as *The Search for the Durotriges* (Oxbow, 2011).

INTRODUCTION

A TUDOR ESTATE SURVEY OF THE ISLE OF PURBECK, WITH MAPS, 1585-1586

THIS BOOK REPRODUCES, describes, transcribes and sets in context a volume of maps and written surveys preserved among the muniments of the Bankes family of Kingston Lacy, Dorset. It was made for and belonged to one of Queen Elizabeth I's most important courtiers, Sir Christopher Hatton. The purpose of the survey was to provide an account of his lands in Dorset and Ralph Treswell was in the first generation of English estate surveyors to produce maps to accompany their written texts.

The Dorset coast is shown here just before the launch of the Spanish Armada from Catholic Spain against Protestant England, which would appear in the summer of 1588. This political context adds a national defensive aspect to the survey of this area at a critical moment. Important, too, are the depictions of Corfe Castle showing this ancient stronghold intact, before its destruction in the Civil War some sixty years later, providing a unique picture of this historically important building.

This detailed description and depiction of Hatton's Dorset lands, especially by reproduction of the maps in colour, reveals what these places looked like in the late sixteenth century, and together with the written survey, tells us who lived there and how they farmed these lands.

Bound in with Treswell's maps and surveys are a map of the county of Dorset by Christopher Saxton, one of his series of county maps, and a map of the lands of the Daccombe family in Corfe Castle by the relatively unknown cartographer John Hawsted. This latter map is dated to the early seventeenth century, taking the history of this survey beyond the time of its commissioner, as Sir Christopher Hatton died on 20 November 1591.

SIR CHRISTOPHER HATTON

RALPH TRESWELL'S SURVEY of Corfe Castle and lands in the Isle of Purbeck was commissioned by Sir Christopher Hatton. Born in 1540, Hatton rose swiftly from a background of lesser Northamptonshire gentry to become a student of law at the Inner Temple by 1560. From this base he became a regular figure within the court of Elizabeth I where he was noted as a gifted dancer. He also showed the makings of a loyal statesman and diplomat. The Elizabethan court presented many opportunities for gifted and ambitious men, and Christopher Hatton seized his chance.[1]

Hatton's list of public appointments shows his meteoric rise from provincial gentleman to national grandee. He became a Member of Parliament for Northamptonshire in 1571, a gentleman of the Privy Chamber in 1572, Vice-Chamberlain of the Royal Household in 1577, the year he was knighted, and Lord Chancellor in May 1587. These positions at court kept Hatton in London for the majority of the time, as his letter book of 1579 shows that he can not have been away from Elizabeth's court for any period longer than one week in that year.[2]

There was a heavy price to pay to maintain such a high profile in public and at the court. In the sixteenth century, gentlemen would speculate to accumulate, and Hatton's rise to prominence was accompanied by extravagant gestures, displays and purchases. His list of property acquisitions included Kirby Hall near Corby in Northamptonshire in 1575, and from 1580 he embarked on the construction of a magnificent house at Holdenby, the estate he inherited in the same county. Hatton acquired a suitable London base in the former palace of the Bishop of Ely in Holborn beside the eponymous Hatton Garden.

He was granted the Isle of Purbeck in 1572 by the Crown, for a steep fee of £4,671, which together with his ambitious building programmes elsewhere, put him in debt for the rest of his life.

Sir Christopher Hatton. Unknown artist, circa 1588-91. National Portrait Gallery, ref,1518.

HATTON IN DORSET

THIS VOLUME LOOKS specifically at the survey and the maps of Christopher Hatton's Dorset estates, which were part of a wider survey of the estates Hatton had inherited and purchased in Northamptonshire, his main base, for which he had started to commission survey work from the early 1580s.

In 1572 Hatton became Keeper of Corfe Castle, and Admiral of the Isle of Purbeck. The Spanish Armada would not set sail for sixteen years, but it was clear that raids from the Continent and even threat of invasion were current concerns through these years. Hatton, as Privy Councillor and the Queen's man, was a reliable deputy who could be trusted to manage the important strongpoint of Corfe Castle. In 1576 he increased his naval authority with the acquisition of Brownsea Castle on Brownsea Island, which Henry VIII built from 1545-1547 to defend the strategic anchorage within Poole Harbour. The importance of Hatton's role as guardian of these southern coastal defences and of Corfe Castle was clear to his contemporaries.

In the early 1580s Hatton added the Purbeck manors of Studland and Langton Wallis, but since the majority of his lands were in Northamptonshire, and he spent most of his time in London, Hatton would not be drawn into the local politics of the Dorset gentry families. Much of the daily management of the Purbeck estate was left to his trusted deputy Francis Hawley who styled himself Vice-Admiral and was elected as a Member of Parliament for Corfe Castle in 1572, 1586 and 1588.

Holdenby House, Northamptonshire

SIXTEENTH-CENTURY SURVEYING

WHY WAS THE survey made, and why was it made with maps? When Hatton acquired his Dorset properties and offices he needed a guide to his new lands. A survey would show their extent and the rents they brought in, as well as any rights, privileges, customs and obligations with regard to his tenants. All of these aspects of the estate would have been known to his steward and recorded in various documents, such as rentals, surveys, manor court rolls, accounts and perambulations, but not in a single work of reference.

Hatton's social position required constant display and demonstration. It was not enough to hold lands and offices: his friends and rivals needed to know about his acquisitions, and this information should be presented to them in the most attractive, impressive and up-to-date manner available. Hatton wanted a written survey illustrated with maps, which by the 1580s were beginning to be drawn by professional mapmakers, and it was fashionable and useful to have one's estates portrayed in this way. This was not just true of Hatton's Dorset estate, but also of his lands in Northamptonshire and his London property. The survey and maps at once provided summary documents detailing all of his possessions as well as high quality display objects to demonstrate his extensive lands to contemporaries.

The frontispiece to the volume bears the coat of arms of Sir Christopher Hatton surmounted by the symbol of the Golden Hind, a name made famous when Francis Drake used it to rename his ship the *Pelican* in honour of the patron of his exploratory voyages.[3] Drake and the *Golden Hind* captured a Spanish treasure ship during the first circumnavigation of the world and this piece of good fortune added considerably to Hatton's wealth as well as to his prestige. Hatton's coat of arms, beautifully hand-painted, presumably by Ralph Treswell drawing on his painter-stainer background, symbolises Hatton's ownership of this estate – an estate represented in the volume through the power of the written word and the new concept of the map, visually making clear the bounds, contents and value of the lord's domains. Hatton, a largely absentee landlord, could thus symbolically hold his estate in his hand by taking this volume off the shelf in the library of his London or Northamptonshire house, and leafing through the pages, he could in his mind's eye visit his Dorset estate, and show it to his many illustrious visitors.

RALPH TRESWELL THE ELDER, SURVEYOR AND MAPMAKER

CHRISTOPHER HATTON commissioned surveys of his Northamptonshire and Dorset estates from Ralph Treswell, who had been in his employ since 1571. Who was Ralph Treswell? or rather, who was Ralph Treswell *the elder*, since he had a mapmaker son of the same name, who signed himself 'junior'?

Treswell's early life and career are not well documented, but from later evidence it appears that he was born between October 1542 and April 1543.[4] He was thus aged about 25 when his work first appears on record in 1567-1568, about 38 when he drew his first surviving map, about 42 when he began work on this Dorset estate survey, and 74 when he died in 1616.

Treswell is first recorded making a banner and streamers for the Carpenters' Company. This places him by trade among the Painter-Stainers, a London-based fraternity in the records of which he appears as a trustee from 1580, and whose work included among other things heraldic painting of coats of arms and other emblematic material for display purposes, and house painting.[5] The Painter-Stainers' Company was involved in processions, displays and ceremonial activities at the Tudor court: painted cloths hung from walls, stained glass windows illuminated rooms and decorated plaster covered the walls of buildings. Treswell's work as a painter-stainer and member of the company was likely therefore to have brought him into contact with court circles.

Treswell is recorded in the service of Christopher Hatton from 1571, and from 1580 he started to make written surveys and maps of Hatton's estates. He was noted as a resident of Aldersgate in London from 1577, and began to undertake commissions for plans of London properties from 1585 and continued with these intermittently until 1614, two years before his death.[6]

THE LATER HISTORY OF THE SURVEY

WHEN SIR CHRISTOPHER HATTON died on 20th November 1591 his heir was his nephew William, son of his sister Dorothy (b.1536 - d.1591) and John Newport of Hunnington (d. 1565). William Newport adopted the surname of Hatton in order to inherit from his uncle, but did not enjoy his inheritance for long as he died only five years later in 1596, perhaps weighed down by the associated debts. He left no son and his Northamptonshire lands eventually passed to a cousin, John Hatton of Stanton, Cambridgeshire. Lady Elizabeth Hatton, wife of William, inherited rights to her first husband's Purbeck Estate which she retained after her second marriage to Edward Coke, Chief Justice of the Commons Pleas. On the death of Edward Coke in 1634 Elizabeth felt free to dispose of her Purbeck property which she sold to Sir John Bankes in 1635.[7]

Although Sir Christopher Hatton's family did not retain the lands in Purbeck, the survey he commissioned was important to later generations. It is likely to have acted as a sales catalogue in 1635 when Sir John Bankes purchased Corfe Castle, Studland, Langton Wallis and the rest of the lands formerly held by Hatton. Once bound into its most recent format it was subsequently presented as evidence before the Court of Chancery on several occasions and in a 19th century Admiralty case to determine the ownership of barrels of brandy washed up in a shipwreck.

The survey provides an insight into the ancient use of lands in Purbeck, the archaic structures and customs that were still in practice in the sixteenth century. It gives an extraordinary illustration of Corfe Castle intact, fifty years before its destruction in the English Civil War, and a rare insight into the lands, rents, rights and responsibilities associated with the lands of a significant figure within the Elizabethan court.

1   Hatton's life as a courtier is well documented by an edition of his political correspondence Nicolas, H. (ed.) *Memoirs of the Life and Times of Sir Christopher Hatton, K. G., Vice-Chamberlain and Lord Chancellor to Queen Elizabeth: Including Correspondence with the Queen and other Distinguished Persons,* London, 1847, and three monograph biographies: Brooks, E. St. J. *Sir Christopher Hatton: Queen Elizabeth's Favourite,* London, 1946, is a very detailed and well researched narrative, Vines, A. G. *Neither Fire Nor Steel: Sir Christopher Hatton,* Chicago, 1978, provides a critical assessment of Hatton as a politician, Deacon, M. *The Courtier and the Queen: Sir Christopher Hatton and Elizabeth I,* Northampton, 2008, places Hatton in the context of the county gentry and makes extensive use of locally held records.
2   http://www.historyofparliamentonline.org/volume/1558-1603/member/hatton-christopher-i-1540-91 accessed 23/6/2017
3   Deacon *The Courtier and the Queen*, pp. 108-111.
4   Treswell stated his age while giving evidence in a number of Chancery cases, Gerhold, D. 'New light on Ralph Treswell', in *London Topographical Record* volume 31, publication number 176, 2015, pp. 45-49.
5   Schofield, J. *The London surveys of Ralph Treswell,* London Topographical Society Publication no. 135, 1987, p.1.
6   Schofield, *The London surveys of Ralph Treswell,* pp. 1-5
7   Bankes, G. *The Story of Corfe Castle,* London, 1853, p. 56.

THE ARCHAEOLOGY AND HISTORIC LANDSCAPE EVIDENCE WITHIN RALPH TRESWELL'S MAPS

IN THIS CHAPTER the maps are examined for their archaeological and historic landscape evidence.

They are remarkably detailed for their time and demonstrate that much of Purbeck's countryside: the roads, paths and trackways, woodlands, field systems, farmsteads, settlements and boundaries, had largely been established by Elizabeth I's reign. They also reveal information relating to industry, land tenure and hunting.

In 1585 Sir Christopher Hatton commissioned a trusted professional, Ralph Treswell, to survey his newly acquired Corfe Castle Estate. He wanted to see and understand what he owned, his rights and privileges and the income that could be generated from his land.

It took thirteen years for Hatton to purchase the various properties and assemble the Corfe Castle Estate and following his death in 1591 the land was left to his nephew William. It was sold to Sir John Bankes by William's widow Elizabeth in 1635 and remained in the Bankes family until 1981 when it was bequeathed to the National Trust.

My first direct contact with Ralph Treswell's maps was in 1986 when I was asked by the National Trust to carry out a historic landscape and archaeological survey for the Corfe Castle Estate.

I had heard of Treswell's maps of Corfe Castle and village, which had been reproduced in black and white by the Royal Commission on Historical Monuments, but was surprised to learn that there were further maps to be examined.[1]

In 1981 Mr H.J.R Bankes left his Dorset estates, comprising 16,000 acres of land in Purbeck and East Dorset, to the National Trust. This included the ruins of Corfe Castle but also the mansion of Kingston Lacy with its nationally significant collections. Cupboards in the house held the Bankes family archive which was of such value that it was quickly transferred to the Dorset Record Office (now Dorset History Centre) to be preserved in a purpose built archival strongroom. Among the papers was a leather bound book containing Treswell's maps.

I booked a table and drove down to Dorchester to begin the research. I remember the anticipation when handed the survey. I opened the cover and turned to the first page. There was Christopher Saxton's 1575 map of Dorset with its general representation of the county and scatter of named places, churches and deer parks.

This level of mapping was really all an archaeologist could expect from a Tudor map of Dorset, as more detailed mapping is very rare for this period. I have carried out landscape surveys in west Dorset where the 1840s parish tithe map is the earliest large-scale survey of a place. In these circumstances, it is possible to work from the 19th century list of field names and trace them back through older inventories in the hope of understanding how present field systems and farms have developed through time.

If you are lucky there is an 18th century estate map: many enlightened land owners decided to have their property surveyed during this period and they are reasonably common. The Corfe

Castle Estate is doubly fortunate in having both detailed 16th- and 18th-century maps, as Henry Bankes commissioned William Woodward to conduct such a survey for his Kingston Lacy and Corfe Castle Estates 1773-1775.[2] Far fewer and generally less detailed maps exist for the 17th century but I found the third map in the Treswell survey volume to be a bonus. This was a map by John Hawsted which shows Corfe Castle and village. It is particularly valuable because it reveals structural changes to the Castle before its demolition in 1646.

The second map in the book sets the scene. This is Treswell's guide map for the whole of Purbeck on which he displayed the lands of his client Sir Christopher Hatton. Treswell shaded Hatton's manors orange-brown to distinguish them from the rest and on each of these areas he drew a deer, perhaps to represent the golden hind prominent on Hatton's family crest.

Hatton had been building his Purbeck empire since 1572, when he purchased the great fortress of Corfe Castle from Elizabeth I. The command of Brownsea Castle in Poole Harbour was granted to him in 1576 and in 1582 Elizabeth sold him the north-east coastal manor of Studland. Sir Christopher completed his estate in April 1585 when he purchased the manors of Langton Wallis and Eastington centred on the south Purbeck limestone plateau. Langton Wallis included a separate block of land, Middlebere, a large area of heathland jutting out into Poole Harbour north of Corfe Castle.[3]

Treswell seems to have begun his Purbeck work soon after the Langton purchase, as this is his earliest dated map in the survey book. Corfe village with Bucknowle were also surveyed in 1585 and the other dated maps were completed in 1586.

Hatton's Corfe Castle Estate largely matched that bequeathed to the National Trust 400 years later. Newton and Afflington had been sold long before the 20th century, although the maps for both appear in Treswell's volume. Similarly, Ailwood, included in the Langton Wallis map, and Bucknowle Farm, detailed on the Corfe map, had to be sold by Sir Ralph Bankes in the late 17th century.[4] Money was in short supply following the financial upheavals of the Civil War and funds were needed to build Ralph's new fashionable house at Kingston Lacy. The only other difference to Hatton's estate was the manor of Godlingston, purchased by John Bankes in 1765.[5] Treswell noted that it belonged to a Mr Welles in 1586.

Having seen Saxton's and Hawsted's surveys, followed by the Purbeck map, the fourth drawing in the book causes a sharp intake of breath: the detailed measured plan of Corfe Castle. This, when taken with the Hawsted map, as well as the fifth map in the book, that of castle and village, comprise the only known illustrations of the layout of the whole Castle before its demolition.

Sir John Bankes was a loyal supporter of King Charles I and Corfe became a Royalist stronghold. Following its capture in 1646, the Parliamentary sappers set out to deny the enemy this fortress and in the demolition process, obscured the details of its buildings and defences. Ralph Treswell's plan is an invaluable guide to how it would have looked in Hatton's time (see below).

Turning the pages beyond Corfe village, I found cartography beyond expectation. I had no idea that each of Hatton's manors would have a detailed written inventory of tenancies with names, areas of land, manorial rights and dues. Each accompanied by their vibrantly drawn maps: Afflington and Newton, Eastington and Langton Wallis, Middlebere and Studland; each a visual time capsule of the Elizabethan age.

Therefore, in 1986, my day in the record office was time well spent, enabling me to see the Corfe Castle Estate in extraordinary detail. Treswell is an illustrated fixed point, both to locate earlier written information and to compare the Tudor historic landscape with the future Georgian Woodward survey maps of 1775. On that day, I wrote notes and took photographs so that I could record and analyse the information the maps contained. Now, we have sophisticated computers and high resolution scans enabling us to zoom at will into small cartographic detail.

1986 was exciting but in 2016 I was surprised by a second revelation. I was sent scans of Treswell's sister survey book held at the Northamptonshire Record Office. This is equally amazing and demonstrates that Ralph Treswell had already been working for Sir Christopher since 1580.

THE PURBECK MAPS AND THE NORTHAMPTONSHIRE SURVEY

TRESWELL'S MAPS DEPICT the Hatton family estate and include the Northamptonshire lands of Kettering, Church and Chapel Brampton, Deane, Thorpe, Bennefield and Elkington. The best maps relate to Holdenby which Hatton had inherited from his father. Three of Treswell's maps dated 1580, 1584 and 1587 demonstrate how Sir Christopher transformed the area. The 1580 map shows a great, newly erected house referred to as Holdenby Palace, it was as big as Hampton Court and the largest privately owned residence in the country.[6]

Extract from Treswell 1580 Holdenby map showing Holdenby Palace and the site of the old manor house beside the church.

The map shows the parish church isolated within an enclosure. It is common to see villages removed to make way for 18th-century parks and gardens but Treswell shows an example from the 16th century. Hatton's old family home once stood next to the church but this had been swept away by Sir Christopher's grand scheme. The historian and archaeologist in Treswell helpfully marks the position of the old building with the words 'here stode ye manor house'. By 1587 the ornate gardens with ponds, warren and deer park were complete but the manor house site was preserved within an enclosed corner of the park and Treswell helpfully marks out the footings as dotted lines.

The 1584 map shows the south part of Holdenby deer park and rabbit warren. The wooden park paling is shown and the deer are clearly depicted as fallow deer (the typical species chosen for enclosed deer parks) in contrast to the red deer depicted on the Purbeck maps. This part of the park had been enclosed out of the fields of Church and Chapel Brampton. Perhaps there was local resentment and a risk of poaching as Treswell drew a keeper patrolling the park with two dogs on a lead and what appears to be a musket resting on his shoulder. Treswell's people are shown on several of his maps. He depicts ordinary men dressed in their working clothes carrying the tools of their trade.

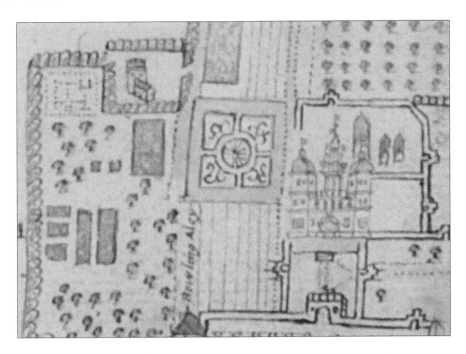

Extract from Treswell's 1587 map showing Holdendby Palace and additional garden detail with the old manor house beside the church marked out with dotted lines.

left: Detail from Treswell's 1584 Church and Chapel Brampton map showing fallow deer and keeper with dogs.
right: Detail of Treswell's 1580 survey of Cottingham Woods and Benefeelde Park showing crossbow man and fallow deer.

On the Northampton Benefeelde map, the deer park lodge is shown with two men holding crossbows, perhaps for culling the deer that surround them in the deer park enclosure.

In Purbeck, three men are shown on the Middlebere map, each carrying tools. Two men carry different types of cutting tools with a hooked point, these were probably used for cutting the heathland furze or gorse for livestock feed and fuel for heating bread ovens.

Details from Treswell's 1586 map of Middlebere showing men with tools probably for furze cutting

The other man stands in the east part of Middlebere with a long pole, amongst rabbits. Perhaps he is a warrener overseeing the land management as Tudor rabbit farming was a lucrative business and the stock required maintenance, feeding and guarding.

THE FREE WARREN OF PURBECK

F ROM MEDIEVAL TIMES, the whole of Purbeck was a free warren in which two warreners and a ranger were employed. They were managed by the steward and constable of Corfe Castle and these in turn were representatives of the king. Treswell copied out the rights, liberties and customs of the warren which had been transferred to Hatton by Elizabeth I as 'contayned in the olde charter'. These writings demonstrate that the Warren of Purbeck was more than a place to farm rabbits and included a range of privileges that provided status, power and wealth to the owner.

Hunting land in the medieval period was the preserve of the rich and hunting rights were granted by the king. The royal forests were the king's hunting land in which the beasts of the forest, the deer and the wild boar, were reserved. Chases were areas of private forest land in which the aristocracy were given royal permission to hunt the beasts of the forest. A park was an area of land which the king allowed a lord of a manor to enclose for deer (like that shown on the Benefeelde and Holdenby maps).

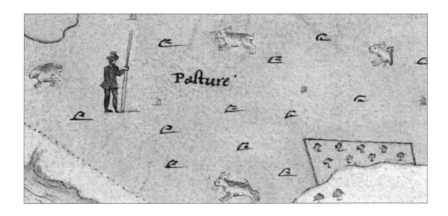

Detail from Treswell's 1586 map of Middlebere showing a rabbit warren and a man carrying an implement of unknown use

A right of free warren could be granted by the king to a lord to allow him to hunt the smaller game across his estate. In the medieval period, the animals of the warren included the fox, the hare, the rabbit, the wildcat, the pheasant and the partridge. This was distinct from a warren which was an enclosed area of land used particularly for breeding and hunting rabbits.[7] It seems that by 1586, eastern Middlebere had become a warren of this type.

Purbeck is unusual in that it is described as a free warren but has rights normally attached to a royal forest. In fact, early 13th-century documents indicate that Purbeck originated as a forest and King John came to hunt there.[8]

Another heathland occupation was turf cutting for fuel, though none of the Treswell's Middlebere men seem to be holding a turfing spade. However, the written survey pages accompanying the Langton Wallis map describe the 'right to cut turf north of the gallows and east of the porte way as far as thorne moor' and the Middlebere map shows where this land was as the position of the gallows beside the road to Wareham is clearly shown.

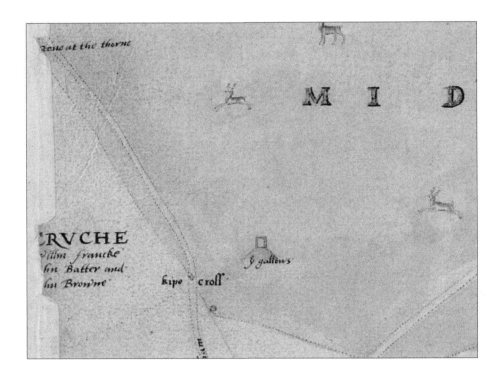

Detail from Treswell's 1586 map of Middlebere showing the road from Corfe to Wareham and the gallows.

THE CASTLE

CORFE CASTLE, DESPITE its 17th century ruination, is still one of the great medieval royal castles of Britain. This fortress is particularly significant for its 11th-13th century architecture with its cutting-edge military design. It occupies a central point on the chalk Purbeck ridge which forms a natural rampart across the centre of the Island. In geological time, water courses cut the ridge and isolated Castle Hill. It became a naturally defensive position to guard the Corfe gap, the only easily accessible route through the Purbeck Hills.

This landscape setting would always have been important and we found struck prehistoric flint and Roman pottery during excavations at the Castle, evidence that it has long been a focus of activity.[9]

The Castle is divided into three main enclosures: the Inner Ward (Treswell's Third and Fourth Wardes) containing the principal buildings including the royal apartments; the West Bailey (Treswell's Second Ward) containing the accommodation of the constable, who in medieval times would have managed the affairs of the castle for the king in his absence; the Outer Bailey (Treswell's First Warde) would have contained the workshops and stables of the castle.

The site, particularly the West Bailey, was occupied in the Saxon period and by 1086 had been acquired from Shaftesbury Abbey by William I.[10] The original tower keep on the summit of the hill may initially have been constructed of wood but in the early 12th century, Henry I had this rebuilt in stone (the 'Kinges Tower' on Treswell). The stone wall surrounding the Inner Ward is also Norman as are the remains of the 'old hall' in the West Bailey. The Gloriette (Queenes Tower) on the east side of the Keep was built for King John in the early 13th century. The curtain wall and towers enclosing the West Bailey are also of this date, as are three of the towers on the west side of the Outer Bailey.

The two great gatehouses protected the southern approaches to the Outer Bailey and West Bailey and they were each originally fronted by a drawbridge across a deep ditch. Both were redesigned in the mid-13th century for Henry III, and the Outer Gatehouse was substantially improved for Edward I in the 1280s. Detailed accounts of this period describe the work as weekly itemised payments to named craftsmen, including masons and carpenters.[11]

The other towers in the Outer Bailey date to the mid to late 13th century. Only the Gloriette Tower at the south-east angle of the Inner Ward dates to the 14th century and little additional largescale construction work seems to have taken place at Corfe in the late medieval period.[12]

Fragments of Purbeck limestone window jambs, surviving in the Keep, are remains of the 16th- and 17th-century refurbishments made to the Castle. At this time it was converted from a declining royal fortress to the prestigious mansion of a gentleman. The Hawsted map shows that the Inner Ward south bastion and east turret had been added between 1586 and the 1640s.

From 1986 until 1997, the National Trust conducted archaeological excavations at Corfe Castle to improve access and to display new parts of the ruin. Much architectural detail had become hidden by rubble and vegetation since the castle's 1646 demolition. The accuracy of Treswell's plan of Corfe Castle was proved at the Outer Gatehouse during our first year.[13] We excavated a mound against the curtain wall and found the flight of stone steps leading up to the first floor of the Gatehouse which Treswell shows on his plan.

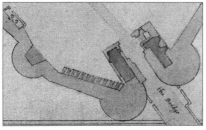

above left: The mound before the excavation

above right: The steps uncovered 1986

left: As shown on Treswell's 1586 plan of Corfe Castle

The Corfe village map shows the Castle in perspective and demonstrates that the drum towers flanking the gateway had domed roofs with a central and higher domed tower above the passage through the Gatehouse. The demolition and subsequent quarrying of stone for reuse has left no evidence of this upper structural detail today.

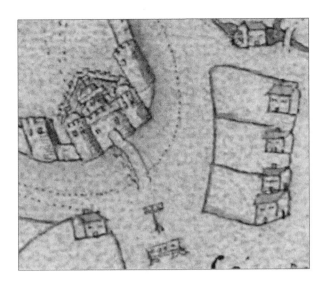

Detail of Treswell's 1585 Corfe village map showing the domed turrets of the Outer Gatehouse opposite the market place stocks and pillory

Within the east curtain wall of the Outer Bailey, the tiled stable block is shown where there is now just a gap, a weak spot undermined by the Parliamentarian sappers in 1646. Other details include latrines shown against the west wall of the Outer Bailey and north wall of the West Bailey and two wells, one in the Outer Bailey and another in the Inner Ward.

Treswell shows that the well in the Inner Ward was probably already old in the 1200s when King John built his stylish manor house, known as the 'Gloriette'. The map shows how the east Gloriette wall narrowed to accommodate the position of the well, thus creating another weak spot where subsequent demolition has obscured this detail.

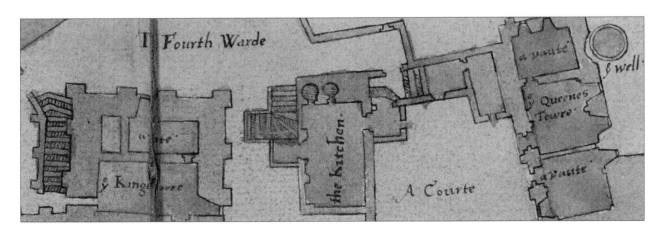

Detail from Treswell's 1586 plan of Corfe Castle showing the relationship between Gloriette (Queenes Towre) and the well (right) and central position of kitchen with two circular ovens. Flights of steps link the kitchen to the neighbouring principal buildings.

Treswell's map reveals that the irregular grass covered earthwork between the two principal buildings of the Inner Ward was once the Castle's kitchen. Flights of stairs linked this kitchen to the Norman keep on the west and King John's Gloriette on the east. Two large ovens are shown built into the north wall.

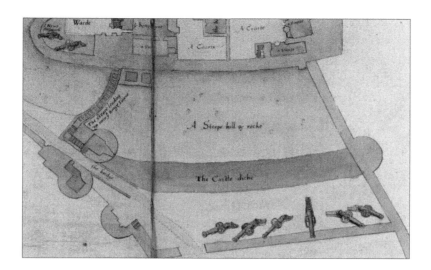

The maps demonstrate a need for defence and early warning against likely invasion. Elizabeth's government was threatened by Spain. The maps were drawn only two years before the great Spanish Armada was launched in its attempt to land an army against Protestant England. Eight cannons are shown on the Corfe Castle plan, two on the 'New Bulwark' facing west above the West Bailey and another six along the upper terrace of the Outer Bailey, south of the 'Castle Diche'.

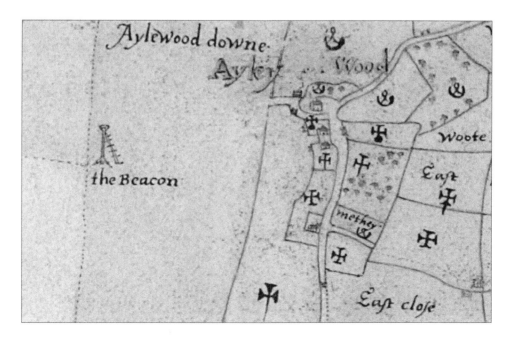

On the Langton Wallis map, a beacon is drawn with a flight of steps up to the fire pot on top of the timber tower. This was one of a chain of coastal signal stations which were located along the south coast to warn of invasion.

THE DOMESDAY MANORS

Tʜᴇ ᴅᴏᴍᴇsᴅᴀʏ ʙᴏᴏᴋ of 1086 records the names of many small Purbeck manors which still survive as farms and settlements in the landscape today.

The Eastington and Langton Wallis map depicts ancient walled boundaries. This southern part of Purbeck is a limestone plateau and the fields are divided by drystone walls. A series of long parallel boundaries divide the land into similar sized units. These extend from the coastal cliffs, north to the ancient route known as the Priest's Way. Treswell shows this track and repeats some of the Domesday names demonstrating that these ancient landholdings still existed in his time. By the 13th century, Ailwood, Wilkswood and Acton had been absorbed into the west Langton manor held by the Wallis family as distinct from east Langton manor held by members of the Matravers family.

Treswell shows the walled division between the manors of Eastington and Acton and this wall remains today as the boundary between Worth Matravers and Langton Matravers parishes. The next long boundary east divides Acton from Langton Wallis and the next divides Langton Wallis from Langton Matravers manor (in contrast to the parish name which combines the areas of both manors Langton Wallis and Matravers).

Treswell shows, on a separate map, one more of these ancient manorial units. It lies further east as a detached piece of Langton Wallis. Treswell describes it as part of 'Langton Farm' but it may have been the Domesday manor of 'Thorne' as two of its fields are named Great Thorne Close and Little Thorne Close. Today this land is known as Verney Farm and is still a distinct unit of land enclosed by the same boundaries as shown on Treswell's map. Treswell shows no buildings on 'Langton Farm' but elsewhere he shows buildings where farms and hamlets still stand.

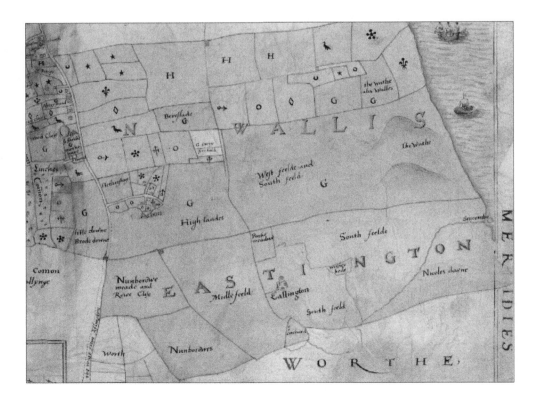

Details from Treswell's 1585 Langton Wallis & Eastington maps showing the long boundaries dividing ancient Domesday manors (Worth, Eastington, Acton, Langton) and the separate enclosed block of land known as Langton Farm.

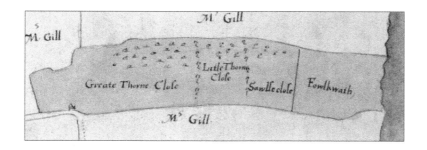

WOODS AND QUARRIES

THE PURBECK LIMESTONE is a good building material and farm houses and cottages still contain ancient fabric. Wilkswood for example, another Domesday manor, retains a medieval window splay in the west gable of the farmhouse.

Wilkswood differs from other Purbeck farmsteads because by the 13th century it had become a small monastic foundation which included a manorial chapel dedicated to St Leonard. It was a chantry by 1314, where masses were to be said daily for the family of the manorial lord, John le Waleys and his family. The monastic records, the Wilkswood Cartulary, provide details for this place dating back to the 13th century.[14] One of these documents describes a grant of land known as 'Berneswod' given by Alured de Lincoln 'to the church of St Leonard which is in Wilkswood'. The document mentions that the field was surrounded by a ditch in 1240.[15] Treswell marks the position of Barneswood and shows that 445 years later the land was still farmed from Wilkswood as it is marked with an H representing the 1580s Wilkswood tenants, the Havelland family. The closure of the English monastic houses by Henry VIII and his son Edward VI, meant that by the 1540s Wilkswood had ceased to be a priory and the land had been transferred to farm tenants.[16]

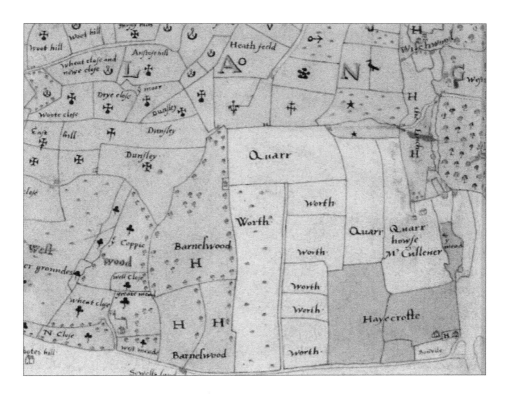

Detail from Treswell's 1585 Langton Wallis and Eastington map showing Wilkswood and Langton West (top right), Barneswood (centre) and West Wood (bottom left)

Immediately south of Wilkswood Farm is woodland. Treswell names it East Wood and West Wood and today the same area is named Talbot Wood and Langton West Wood. Entering through the trees, you soon understand why the land has remained wooded. It is deeply pitted by quarries. This land coincides with the outcropping of the Burr Stone and Pubeck Marble beds which were much valued in the medieval and Roman periods.[17]

The Burr stone was a free stone and much of Corfe Castle is built of this. It does not fracture along bedding planes and therefore can be freely worked in all directions. When freshly quarried, it was supposed to be as soft as butter 'beurre' to work but over time hardened on exposure to weathering. The qualities of this bed of stone are demonstrated in the sound condition of Corfe Castle as we see it today, despite its ruination almost 400 years ago.

Purbeck Marble became fashionable in the 13th and 14th centuries for decorative architectural detail. Although this geological bed is a limestone, it takes a polish like marble. It is found in many medieval churches including Salisbury Cathedral and Westminster Abbey. At Salisbury this dark stone can be seen as rounded columns decorating the pillars of the nave. Purbeck Marble rots when exposed to weathering and was therefore generally used to decorate the interiors of buildings.

These narrow beds of stone proved so popular that their surface outcrops had largely been worked out by the 15th century, leaving an industrial landscape which was difficult to farm and therefore woodland became the alternative.

The ancient woods include pollarded oaks, where large limbs were grown and harvested for beams and roof trusses; the Wilkswood priests were given rights of 'housebote' for this purpose.[18] Much of the woodland is coppice where stands of hazel rods have been cut and allowed to grow back over the centuries. Stands of hazel were cut in rotation to allow a harvest each year. They have a variety of uses including roof rafters, fencing posts and hurdles. The cut stumps are known as coppice bowls and the larger the diameter, the older the tree. Some of the West Wood coppice bowls must be very ancient. They overlie the yet more ancient quarries which in turn cut through abandoned farming lynchets, terraced long ago into the now wooded slopes.

The Wilkswood Cartulary describes the 13th century arable strip fields granted to the monastic community by the then owner Alured de Lincoln within the open field furlongs of 'Langeton' named as 'Wichwenitnere', 'Heldeaweste', 'Lamesacreste' and 'Litlecroeste'. Though in Langton Wallis common fields had been enclosed by Treswell's time, Studland still retained its open field system.[19]

AGRICULTURE

THE OPEN OR common field system of agriculture dates back to the later Saxon period and was still widely practised in the 1580s. The Northamptonshire map for Kirby shows a manor where arable strips of differing ownership and tenancy were mixed and scattered across the fields but Treswell shows that a process of rationalisation and enclosure seems to be taking place.

At Corfe, the earthworks of strip fields can still be seen in the West Hawes and a few are still marked by mere stones with the initials of the tenants marked on them. The land is now pasture but ownership is still divided between the National Trust and the Bond family of the Creech Estate.

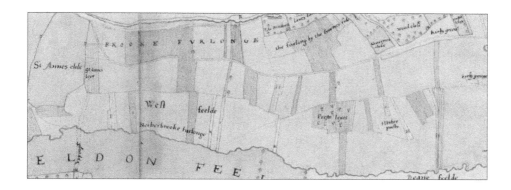

Detail of Treswell's 1584-5 survey of Kirby, Northamptonshire showing the varied ownership and tenancy of arable strips within the open fields.

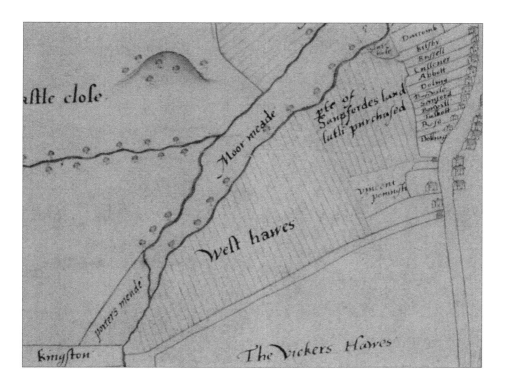

Details of Treswell's 1585 map of Corfe Village showing the strip fields within the common field known as the West Hawes (pronounced locally as halves)

The Studland map shows two large open fields between Studland village and the chalk ridge. A droveway dividing East Feelde from West Feelde linked the village with common grazing on Studland Down (today a public footpath). Within each field Treswell shows the furlong boundaries, each subdivided into parallel strips. They are orientated differently from those within neighbouring furlongs, presumably to limit stripping of topsoil from water run-off during heavy rain. Treswell draws a mound in the East Feelde, and, though it is not named, it is clearly the Bronze Age burial mound still visible today known as the King Barrow.

Between the southern chalk ridge and the northern expanse of Studland Heath, good arable land is limited by geology and topography. The Domesday Book entry for Studland states that in the 11th century it paid tax on three and a half hides. A hide was the Saxon measure of land sufficient to support a household and on the chalk this has been calculated as 120 acres.[20]

Conveniently three and a half times 120 comes to 420, which is almost the same as Treswell's measure of the open fields of Studland at 419 acres and two rods.[21] This is too convenient a calculation but a plausible suggestion given the topographic constraints of the parish mentioned above. The 1775 map shows that the area of the common arable fields had been reduced considerably by this time.[22] The surveyor William Woodward advised his client, Henry Bankes, to improve his income by enclosing what remained; 'it would be better for the whole parish if the Common Fields were inclosed and the Tenants themselves think so and wish it'. By the tithe map survey of 1840 , the open fields were gone.[23]

Detail from Treswell's 1586 map of Studland showing the East and West Common Fields placed on the only good arable land, the chalk between the ridge permanent pasture on the ridge (right) and the village and heathland (left)

Towards the chalk cliffs, at the edge of the West Field, is Studland Wood. Although larger in Treswell's time than it is today, entering the wood reveals evidence that this land has not been cultivated for over 1000 years. The open strip fields never extended this far and instead the earthworks of an older form of farming are hidden by the trees. These are the small rectangular enclosures typical of what are termed 'celtic' fields, in use from the Bronze Age through to the Romano-British period.

Place names can indicate lost features and below Studland Wood, Treswell shows an enclosure named 'Castell Leyes'. This had been divided into three enclosures by 1775 known as 'West Castle', 'East Castle' and 'South East Castle'.[24] The Dorset antiquarian and historian Revd John Hutchins refers to documents claiming that there was once a castle at Studland, where King John stayed in 1205 and 1213.[25] There is another reference to Studland Castle dated 1381.[26] Coker's history, compiled in the early 17th century, mentions a blockhouse here, 'for the more grace named Studland Castle'.[27] This chalk promontory is a good strategic position and there may have been several coastal fortifications built here over the centuries. The castle and blockhouse probably occupied different locations.

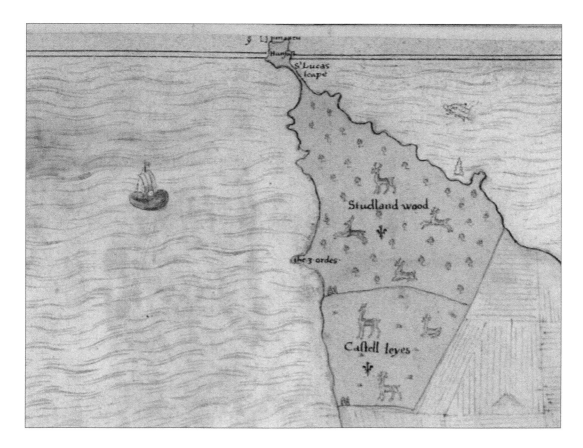

Details from Treswell's 1586 map of Studland showing Studland Wood, Castell Leyes (after a lost castle site?), the mound of the King Barrow bottom right. Note the chalk stacks drawn in the sea and the narrow neck of land which at that time linked the mainland to Hanfast (stronghold) point.

COASTAL CHANGE

TRESWELL ALSO NAMES the western tip of Studland 'Hanfast' which means stronghold. Even in 1586 this area had been severely eroded by the sea with just a narrow bridge of land 'St Lucas Leap' linking it to the mainland. He draws two stacks of chalk jutting out of the sea. The 1586 cliff line when compared to that of today demonstrates the effects of coastal change over 450 years. This change is most dramatic along the Studland shore from South Haven to Little Sea. Treswell shows no sand dunes or beach here and at that time Little Sea was a bay open to the English Channel. Woodward comments on the change in the coastline 'since the old survey'. By 1775 huge amounts of sand had been left here, encircling Little Sea and converting it from an open bay to an inland lake.

Domesday Book refers to thirty-two salt houses operating within Studland manor. This was the biggest salt production site recorded in Dorset and the industry was clearly important in the following centuries.[28] There is little to indicate the importance of the salt industry by 1586 except for the names of two tenements on the shore of Little Sea named 'Salterne' and 'West Salterne'. There were still cottages occupying these sites at that time but by 1775 they had been abandoned.

The Environment Agency has scanned much of Purbeck using LiDAR (Light Detection and Ranging), a modern aerial survey technique that accurately scans the ground surface with laser light impulses to reveal minute undulations in the ground surface. Comparing Treswell's map of Studland with the LiDAR survey demonstrates how accurately he drew his maps.

South Haven peninsula and Greenland Farm to the south have over 100 circular embanked earthworks. These show clearly on a LiDAR survey. These circles are confined to the area of land which existed in Treswell's time and therefore they are most likely to date from a time before the 18th century sand deposition. One explanation for the earthwork circles is that they were evaporating pans for salt production but excavation survey and soil analysis has demonstrated that there is insufficient evidence to support this theory.[29] All that can be said is that there is no known record of their use and that they are probably older than Treswell (who gives no clue that they were in use in the 1580s) and created for some industrial scale process.

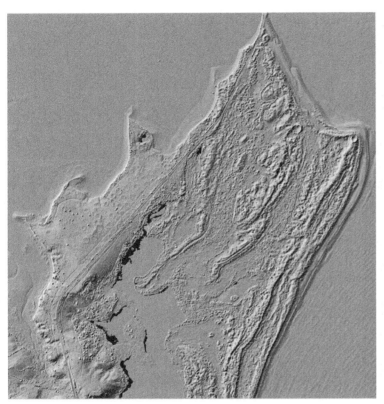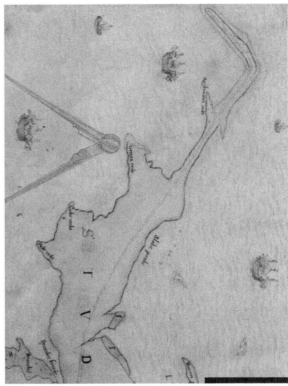

left: The South Haven peninsula in Treswell's time placed beside a 21st century LiDAR image. The 1586 outline of the coast is still clear and demonstrates how accurate Treswell's survey techniques were. Image © The Environment Agency
right: Little Sea was enclosed by the accumulating sand dunes (already in existence by 1775). Note the many earthwork circles on the LiDAR, perhaps pans for salt evaporation, which only exist on the land drawn by Treswell.

The Middlebere map gives more evidence for salt production but in this case the saltworks seem to be still active. Treswell shows two irregular excavations on the coast near Middebere Farmhouse described as 'Salte pitts'.

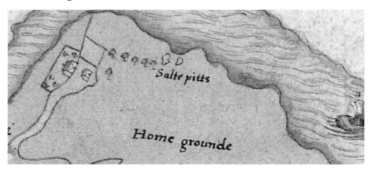

This map evidence is backed up by the written description at the start of Treswell's survey. It records various ancient customary payments due to Corfe Castle from the various Purbeck manors and tithings. Some are to provide money, some fodder hay, others hens but Middlebere, Godlingston, Fitzworth and 'Philpes' were expected to provide annual payments in salt to the castle. These four farms or manors included sections of coast along the south shore of Poole Harbour where historically salt production had taken place. It seems that Middlebere produced the most as it was expected to pay eight times the amount of salt as Godlingston or Philpes.[30] The Treswell survey records that Middlebere was to deliver two quarters or 128 gallons of salt to Corfe annually. However, by 1586, this may have been converted to a money payment of 8s. Treswell's Middlebere map may record the last remnant of the once extensive Roman and medieval salt production industry in Purbeck.

The English Civil War disrupted this pattern of customary payments. After the restoration of the monarchy, Sir Ralph Bankes tried to re-establish his inherited rights in the Courts of Chancery.[31] He used the evidence of Treswell's survey to demand these customary dues from the other Purbeck landowners but had very limited success. By the 1660s, the customs of England were in decline and Corfe's inherited feudal powers proved difficult to enforce.

Thus the Treswell survey gradually moved from a current document to prove legal land rights to a historical record of the way things used to be. But this process was gradual and it was still drawn upon as evidence in determining the customs of Langton Wallis and Wilkeswood in a dispute brought before the Court of Chancery in 1697.[32] As late as 1835 it was used by Willian John Bankes to press his claim in the Court of Admiralty to casks of brandy washed up on the Purbeck beaches.

This chapter has provided a broad sample of the historic land use information that can be extracted from Ralph Treswell's maps. It has concentrated on the land given to the National Trust by the Bankes family and therefore the areas of Newton and Afflington have not been studied. However, the cartographic details highlighted here have, I hope, demonstrated how the maps can guide and illustrate future archaeological and historical research.

Generation by generation, though owners and tenants change, the maps show that the underlying landscape is preserved as evidence of the work of past lives. The countryside is often referred to as a palimpsest, layers of writing on a landscape, sometimes rubbed out to enable new messages to be written but never quite erased. A careful examination enables old messages to be seen below the more recent stories. Treswell's maps give us the confidence to demonstrate this. Beautifully drawn and accurately surveyed, they are illustrations of a time a little beyond the medieval period, when the great changes to society are building, soon to be driven by the agrarian and industrial revolutions of the 17th-19th centuries.

From the lofty heights of Treswell we can peer back towards Domesday and forward into the 21st century.

1 *An Inventory of Historical Monuments in the County of Dorset, volume two, South-East, part 1,* London, 1970, plates 74 and 90.
2 Dorset History Centre, reference D-BKL/E/A/1/13.
3 Hutchins, Rev., J., *The History and Antiquities of the County of Dorset,* third edition, vol. 1, London, 1861-74, p. 644.
4 Dorset History Centre, reference: D-BKL/E/A/3/13.
5 Dorset History Centre, reference: D-BKL/A/B/51.
6 Cherry, B. and Pevsner, N. *The Buildings of England: Northamptonshire,* revised ed.,Harmondsworth, 1973, pp. 263-5.
7 Papworth, M. 'Lodge Farm, Kingston Lacy, Dorset', *Journal of the British Archaeological Association,* 1994, vol. 147, 59-60.
8 Young, C. *The Royal Forests of Medieval England,* University of Pennsylvania Press, 2015, p. 53.

9   Thackray, D. and Papworth, M. 'Corfe Castle, outer gatehouse excavations 1986, Interim report *Proceedings of the Dorset Natural History and Archaeological Society*, 1989, vol.109, p. 114.

10 *An Inventory of Historical Monuments in the County of Dorset, volume two, South-East, part 1*, London, 1970, p. 57.

11 The National Archives, reference: E.101/460/27.

12 *An Inventory of Historical Monuments in the County of Dorset, volume two, South-East, part 1*, London, 1970, pp. 57-78.

13 Thackray, D. and Papworth, M., 1987, 'Corfe Castle, outer gatehouse excavations 1986, Interim report' *Proceedings of the Dorset Natural History and Archaeological Society*, 1991, vol.111, p. 136.

14 Nottingham University, the Middleton Collection, reference: PM/LM 1/1167.

15 Nottingham University, the Middleton Collection, reference: PM/LM 1/1167/6.

16 Page, W., ed., *A History of the County of Dorset*. Vol. 2, London, 1908, p. 98.

17 Dru Drury, G. 'The Use of Purbeck Marble in Medieval Times' *Proceedings of the Dorset Natural History and Archaeological Society*, (1948), vol 65, p. 79. Hutchins, *The History and Antiquities of the County of Dorset*, p. 685, Appendix II.

18 Nottingham University, the Middleton Collection, reference: PM/LM 1/1167/1.

19 Nottingham University, the Middleton Collection, reference: PM/LM 1/1167/7.

20 Grierson, P. 'Weights and Measures' in *Domesday Book Studies*, London, 1987, p. 80.

21 Papworth, M. Studland, Corfe Castle Estate, unpublished archaeological survey for the National Trust, 1995, p. 24.

22 Dorset History Centre, reference: D-BKL/E/A/1/13.

23 Dorset History Centre, reference: T/STD.

24 Dorset History Centre, reference: D-BKL/E/A/1/13.

25 Hutchins, *The History and Antiquities of the County of Dorset*, p. 644.

26 Mills, A., *The Place Names of Dorset* pt 1, English Place Names Society, Nottingham, 1986, vol.52, p. 46.

27 Coker, *A Survey of Dorsetshire Containing the Antiquites*, London, 1732, p. 16. Coker's history is considered to have been written by Thomas Gerrard in the 1620s.

28 Keen, L. 'Medieval Salt Working in Dorset' *Proceedings of the Dorset Natural History and Archaeological Society*, 1988, vol.109, pp. 25-8.

29 Bellamy, P. *Interim Report on the Excavation of Earthwork Circle on Studland Heath*, Poole Harbour Heritage Project, 2010.

30 A bushel of salt was equivalent to 8 gallons and a quarter of salt was 8 bushels.

31 The National Archives, reference: C8/184/13.

32 The National Archives, reference: E 134/9Wm3/East17.

SAXTON, TRESWELL AND HAWSTED: THE MAPS AND CARTOGRAPHERS

INTRODUCTION TO THE MAPS

TEN MAPS ARE interspersed between the text pages of Ralph Treswell's written survey. One is the first map of Dorset as a county, made in 1575 by Christopher Saxton. The remaining nine manuscript maps show specific areas within the Isle of Purbeck estate of Sir Christopher Hatton, for which the written survey was commissioned. Eight maps were made by Ralph Treswell in 1585-1586, which makes these the earliest known estate maps for Dorset. A later map of Corfe manor was drawn by the little-known John Hawsted.

These maps were commissioned in the wider context of Tudor cartography and society against a backdrop of rising awareness of the use and interest of maps, which was evident in the Elizabethan court circles in which Sir Christopher Hatton moved. Maps were gaining importance both as tools for state purposes such as defence and intelligence, while helping to settle matters in legal cases for example over local boundaries, and increasingly seen by landowners as a practical aid for estate management and an opportunity for display.

These maps are examples of exciting new cartographic developments in their time. The map of Dorset was engraved as a separate sheet, and then issued as part of the first atlas of maps of English and Welsh counties, in 1579. The 1580s heralded the emergence of the estate map as a genre, and of professional mapmakers such as Saxton and Treswell. This chapter looks at the details of these Dorset estate maps now that they are all available in print and in colour, to add to our knowledge of the corpus of Treswell's work.

National and local history are here linked in these maps, through the figure of Hatton, the great courtier who commissioned them, and through their wealth of detail, which gives us today an intimate picture of places in the past, providing evidence of both continuity and change in the landscape.

WHY WERE THE MAPS MADE?

THE SURVEY WAS made for Sir Christopher Hatton in the years 1585-1586, following the grant to him of the Corfe Castle estate by Queen Elizabeth I in 1572. Up to this date, and indeed long afterwards, estates were recorded by written survey alone, which listed land parcels with their extent, value and rent. Why were maps made to accompany this particular survey?

A number of factors were at play. Hatton was by this point in his career an influential and powerful figure at court, as a Privy Councillor, and his star was so much in the ascendant that he would become Lord Chancellor in 1587. He is likely to have wanted to use maps to show that he was aware of them as the latest fashion as well as an improved means to administer estates.

The rise of estate maps was to some degree rooted in the Reformation forty years earlier, when monastic lands were seized by the Crown, which then disposed of them by sale or grant to favoured recipients. The new lay owners – often absentee landlords without local knowledge - were concerned to maximise profits from their estates, and maps were a newly-fashionable tool which allowed them to be visualised. They showed where boundaries lay in a clear way which obviated disputes, and conveyed on one sheet the complex relationship of tenants, rents and land use. It was more expensive to have estates mapped as well as surveyed, but the resulting maps had great practical use and also gave an aura of prestige.

Map use in general became increasingly important in court and wider circles from at least the 1580s.[1] This vogue was connected with court officials who were part of Hatton's immediate circle. His close acquaintance, Northamptonshire neighbour and fellow Privy Councillor William Cecil, later Lord Burghley, was influential for decades as Elizabeth's Secretary of State, and made maps himself as well as using them as tools of diplomacy, defence and intelligence.[2] We know that Burghley visited Hatton's house at Holdenby, because he wrote to Hatton about his impressions of the house.[3] Another influence may have been Thomas Seckford, who commissioned the first county maps in the 1570s. In the same way that Seckford ordered this wider survey, it became fashionable for private landowners such as Hatton to commission maps of their estates.

Hatton also knew Dr John Dee, a *savant* well known to Elizabeth I, who may have helped to plan Drake's voyage around the world, and who had a wide correspondence with men of letters across Europe, such as Mercator, who made innovative maps and globes in the later 16th century. Clearly, Hatton was familiar with ideas about the wider importance of geographic knowledge and maps.[4]

The flowering of arts and sciences under Elizabeth I was another factor which favoured map production. Treatises on surveying were published which advised on the use of new methods such as triangulation for accurately measuring area, and on the use of surveying tools such as chain, plane table, and theodolite. It was in the 1580s that this new type of professional surveyor-mapmaker emerged, equipped with the latest tools and able to draw maps to scale. These men signed their maps as advertisements for their skills, and took on commissions.[5]

Ralph Treswell was one of these surveyors, as was Christopher Saxton, who went on to make manuscript maps in the 1590s, after his success with the county maps.[6] As is the case with the Dorset maps in this volume, many estate maps were made by men with the necessary skills, but who came from out of county. Ralph Treswell lived in London; John Hawsted who made the later Corfe map appears to have come from Northamptonshire, while Saxton was born in Yorkshire.

THE COUNTY MAP OF DORSET BY CHRISTOPHER SAXTON, 1575

CHRISTOPHER SAXTON IS a notable example of the new breed of surveyor. In 1573 Saxton was appointed by Thomas Seckford, an important court official acting on behalf of Queen Elizabeth I, to survey the English and Welsh counties. He issued the maps between 1574 and 1578, and then compiled them into the first atlas of county maps in 1579. The motivation was at least in part the national interest and fear of invasion which were particularly strong in the 1570s, spurring an acute interest at court in geographical intelligence about the country, and especially in details of coasts where enemies might land. Lord Burghley annotated his proof copy of the Dorset map to show 'dangerous places for landing of men in the county'.[7]

Saxton's maps marked a new standard in surveying, showing place-names and consistently drawn to scale. He used some form of triangulation[8] to produce the original drawings on which the final engraved maps were based. In the margins of the map, outside the border, are traces of plate-marks, the impression of the copper plate when applied to the paper during the printing process. This method allowed multiple copies to be made, so these maps could reach a wide audience, their popularity enhanced by the decoration of ships, sea monster, and coats of arms.

The Dorset map is dated 1575 in the large decorative cartouche at top left which holds the title. It was the sixth county map to be made, after Hampshire and before Devonshire. It is thought that Saxton travelled from east to west across southern England to carry out the survey work on which he based his maps, since these coastal counties were considered to be in the most danger of attack by one of Protestant England's many Catholic enemies.[9]

Latin was the universal language of scholars until well into the eighteenth century, and the common language among the aristocracy for whom these maps were intended. Saxton used English for most of the place names, but Latin for features such as named rivers which have the letters 'flu', short for 'fluvius', the Latin word for river, and islands in Poole Harbour at lower right, marked 'insul', short for 'insula'.

The title reads 'DORCESTRIAE Comitatus Vicinarumque Regionum nova veraq[ue] Descriptio Anno Domin[i] 1575'. This can be translated as 'A new and true map (or description, but in the sense of a visual description) of the county of Dorset and neighbouring regions'.

Other Latin elements are at lower left of the map. A graduated scale bar surmounted by a pair of dividers with a ship between its open arms bears the legend 'Scala Miliarium' to indicate a scale in miles. This translates to a scale in the form of the modern representative fraction of 1: 183,040.[10]

Detail of the scale bar of Saxton's map.

A pair of dividers to the left of the scale bar balanced by a coat of arms at their right demonstrate the mapmaker's artistic sensibilities. The coat of arms are those of Thomas Seckford, who appears to have instigated and financed these surveys, and so was Saxton's patron. Seckford's motto appears beneath his arms, 'Pestis Patriae Pigricies (recte Pigrities)' which can be translated as 'Sloth is the curse of the fatherland'.[11] Below the scale bar is the mapmaker's attribution: 'Christophorus Saxton descripsit'.

Inserted in the decorative frame around the map, in the centre of each side, are the cardinal points in Latin: 'Septentrio', north, at the top; 'Meridies', south, at the lower edge; at left i.e. in the west is 'Occidens', with 'Oriens' in the east.

The title cartouche is surmounted by the Royal Arms, which appear on all the county maps, here with Elizabeth I's heraldic supporters, the lion and dragon. These symbolically represent the Queen's dominion over all these lands. The cartouche is richly decorated with strapwork, urns of flowers, and birds. In the sea at the lower edge sail ships and boats, drawn in such detail that, under magnification, sailors are visible in some of them. Colour was applied to the finished engraving, too, and all these factors enhance the map's appearance, as an attractive as well as informative addition to any gentleman's library.

The map names the adjoining counties of Devonshire (to left), Somersetshire at top, and Wiltshire at top right, with 'Salesburye Plane' - an obvious example of how spelling of place names was often not at this time in the form we recognise today. The furthest points shown on the map are Beer in Devon to the west; Christchurch, then in Hampshire, to the east; and Mere in Wiltshire to the north. Notable towns include Dorchester, Sherborne, Sturminster Newton, Shaftesbury and Wareham. Some town names differ from the version we know today: 'Burport' (Bridport), 'Candelpurse' (Purse Caundle), 'Lechiot Metreuers' (Lytchett Matravers), and 'Sandwiche' (Swanage).

Saxton presents features in a systematic way, using symbols, to give a well-spaced overall impression, comprehensible to the eye. A building with a spire indicates a village or small town, while larger towns have groups of buildings. Castles are denoted by a symbol of two towers joined by a building between: at Portland, Sandsfoot, Branksea (Brownsea) and Corfe, which sprouts several more towers.

Hills are depicted pictorially, either singly as in the large mound of Lambert's Hill at left, or in lines as in the ridge running across the Isle of Purbeck at lower right. The sea and rivers are coloured blue, with bars across rivers to denote bridges. The Fleet appears as a narrow banked-in water channel less pronounced in shape than it appears today, running from Abbotsbury eastwards to flow into Weymouth Bay.

Tree symbols denote wooded areas: Marshwood Vale in the west, Blackmoor Vale left of centre 'the Vaile of Whithart alias Blakemore', Gillingham Forest and Cranborne Chase (top and top right), Holt Forest (centre right). Parks are shown by fences around trees; some are named such as Blagdon Parke top right (the word 'park' is abbreviated by a cross on the descender of the letter 'p').

Saxton's county maps all have north at the top, which influenced a move towards the convention we now take for granted. These maps were engraved on copper plates to enable production of multiple copies and allow for reprinting, to reach a wide audience, so future patrons and mapmakers were both aware of the standards he set. The way that Saxton presented his maps no doubt had a long-lasting influence on mapmaking; these maps were used as the basis for county maps well into the eighteenth century.

ESTATE MAPS

HERE BELOW IS a table of the earliest known English estate maps I have located, compiled from different sources. It demonstrates the importance of these early estate maps by Treswell for Dorset history and for the history of cartography.

While an earlier map of manors around Sherborne in North Dorset dates to the period 1569-1574, it shows lands of more than one owner, so is not an estate map proper. Christopher Hatton is noted on it as lord of the manor of Purse Caundle; the map was not made for Hatton, but it is the earliest linking of his name with a map, a decade before he commissioned his own estate maps.[12]

From about 1580 the estate map genre really developed, with the rise of the professional mapmaker and a vogue for landowners to commission maps. Thus Treswell's maps for Hatton, of which these Dorset maps are part, are early and fine examples of estate maps in the vanguard of the tradition. These are well made, decorative and often detailed maps, linking Dorset to a wave of cartographic innovations emanating from the royal court in London. By contrast, the only other known Dorset estate map also dated to the 1580s, of part of Durweston cum Knighton, is a pen and ink sketch map with detail of use for practical estate management, but not a treasure that the landowner would show off to visitors.

Table of early estate maps

1573	Grindall Painter	Queen Camel, Somerset[13]
1574	Barnard Drake and William Buckberte	Axminster, Devon[14]
1575	Ralph Agas	West Lexham, Norfolk[15]
1576	Israel Amyce or Ames	Belchamp St Paul, Essex[16]
1579	Israel Ames	Plumberow, Essex[17]
1580	Israel Ames	Long Melford, Suffolk[18]
1580-1587	**Ralph Treswell**	**Hatton estates, Dorset and Northamptonshire[19]**
1581	Ralph Agas	Toddington, Bedfordshire[20]
1581	Thomas Clerke	Panworth Hall estate in Ashill, Norfolk[21]
1582	John Darby	Smallburgh, Norfolk[22]
c.1585	Unknown	Durweston cum Knighton, Dorset[23]

RALPH TRESWELL, MAPMAKER

THE BEAUTIFULLY DRAWN and decorative maps in this volume were made by Ralph Treswell. Their examination in this volume, in the context of his written survey of the same estate, extends our knowledge of his work some fifteen years before the London house plans for which he is well known.[24]

Ralph Treswell was recorded in the service of the courtier Sir Christopher Hatton in Northamptonshire by 1571, although in what capacity is not certain.[25] Given Treswell's training as painter-stainer, he may have worked in this capacity on Hatton's building projects on his houses at Kirby or Holdenby which required much decoration, and it may have been through contact with architects there that he learnt how to make plans. Treswell may also have carried out estate management tasks, and in later life referred to himself as 'surveyor of Sr Cristofers lands'. At this date an estate survey required measuring and recording land in writing, and did not usually include maps, and so Treswell may have been appointed as Hatton's surveyor without specifically being commissioned to make maps.[26]

The date range of this series of maps by Treswell suggests that he first mapped in Northamptonshire between 1580 and 1585, which fits the first tranche of his dated maps from this county, presuming that several undated maps fit into this date range. He then appears to have moved to work on Hatton's Dorset estates, since these surveys date from 1585 to 1586.[27] He moved back to Northamptonshire, where he made three further maps for Hatton in 1587, two of them recording changes in the landscape effected by enclosure of lands he had previously mapped in 1580.[28] Schofield mentions a survey by Treswell of Hatton's estate at Wimbledon but this is not listed in Ralph Hyde's table nor mentioned elsewhere.[29]

From 1585 Treswell was also drawing maps and plans for other clients. These were mainly maps of rural estates, or plans of London houses. The former include maps of rural estates belonging to London institutions such as Christ's Hospital and St Bartholomew's Hospital. There are also three plans now in The National Archives: a map of lands in the parishes of St Martin and St Giles in Westminster for a case in the court of Exchequer in 1585, a map of Hailes Abbey in Gloucestershire for another Exchequer case in 1587, and a map made in 1606 of lands in Esher.[30] The earliest commissions for London house plans, from 1585, were in Cheapside and Tothill Street, with his major London surveys carried out 1607-12.[31] Treswell also drew a map of Brittany in 1594, when he apparently accompanied the military captain Sir John Norris on an expedition sent by Elizabeth I in support of the Protestant Henry IV's bid for the French throne.[32]

There is a further, slightly later, Dorset mapping connection with the Treswell family. From 1607 to 1613 Ralph Treswell's son, also called Ralph, surveyed the estates of the 9th Earl of Northumberland in Dorset, as well as in Middlesex, Sussex and Yorkshire.[33]

THE DORSET MAPS

T HESE NINE MANUSCRIPT maps made by Treswell are the first known Dorset estate maps. Christopher Hatton was generally an absentee landlord, so maps were a useful source of information about his lands, which were distributed among a number of tenants, forming a complex landholding pattern. Other landowners' names written across lands they owned combine with Hatton's holdings to give a picture of ownership across the peninsula.

The maps are bound into the volume with pages of the text survey to which they relate. They do not have titles, but appear after a page naming the area for which the surveys and map follow. This suggests that they were designed for inclusion in a volume. Text boxes on the maps add, or summarise, information about tenants and rents, making this easier to use and so supplementing the written survey. The Studland and Langton Wallis maps use a complex system of symbols to denote land parcels held by different tenants, explained in a key. Confusingly, the same symbols are used on both maps, but not for the same people. The Langton table differentiates between types of tenants using capital letters, which together with the symbols, on a map showing much detail of fields, makes the map hard to read.

Detail of the Langton Wallis map showing symbols and letters used to denote the holdings of different tenants.

The first of Treswell's maps in the volume is an overview of the Isle of Purbeck. It has the same stylistic features as the other maps but it is at a smaller scale, so it shows a larger area in a similar size of map. It acts as a key to the other maps, using a green-brown colour to denote Hatton's lands, which are all included on this map and in the written survey, though not all manors have detailed maps.[34] There is no explanation on the map about this, but it would have been apparent to Hatton and his estate steward, the people most likely to be viewing this map.

It seems likely that Treswell had the Saxton county map in front of him when he made this map; at top right Treswell wrote 'Parte of Wiltshire', which is the legend in the top right corner of Saxton's county map of Dorset. Treswell's map has a similar outline shape to the Saxton map, but more refined details, and differences in outline and placement of some features indicate that it was drawn from Treswell's own survey or from another, more detailed map than Saxton's.

The usual word for a manuscript map at this date, when it was still a relatively rare commodity, was a 'plot'. So where Treswell refers to 'this plot' for example in text on the Corfe Castle map, he means 'this map', rather than a plot of land.

The Treswell maps or plots exhibit stylistic features common to many estate maps, with borders containing cardinal points, text boxes for the title and explanatory notes, and scale bars with dividers. They look similar in style to the county map of Christopher Saxton, and to Saxton's later manuscript maps.[35]

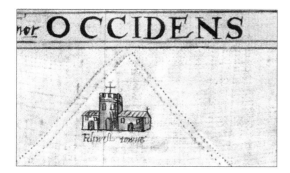

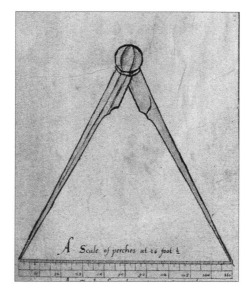

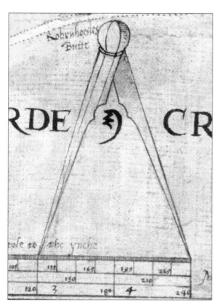

above left: Detail of TNA MPC 1/75 Methwold Warren, John Lane, 1580

above right: Detail of Corfe Castle manor, Ralph Treswell, 1585

below left: Detail of TNA MPC 1/75 Methwold Warren, John Lane, 1580

below right: Detail of Treswell's Newton Heath map, Ralph Treswell, 1585

There is also a similarity between Treswell's Dorset maps and John Lane's map of Methwold Warren in Norfolk of 1580.[36] The pairs of dividers over the scale bars and the cardinal points are areas of particular agreement. Another example similar to Treswell's maps is that of a map of the Fenland between Peterborough and Wisbech, by John Hexham of Huntingdon made in about 1590.[37] The maps by Treswell, then, are stylistically part of a map genre which is evident across mapmakers and maps of different areas of the country through the 1580s and 1590s.

Estate maps rarely showed the complete landscape, but were limited to those aspects that specific circumstances demanded. They merely sketched lands beyond the bounds of the estate in question. When viewing estate maps we need to bear in mind that they do not show every detail of the landscape even within the specified lands, just those which were pertinent for the estate or to the landowner. It is interesting that Treswell's depiction of Corfe on his area map includes a pillory and stocks in the town square. Perhaps they were depicted as items of general interest, or they may relate to Hatton's role as lord of the manor. Estate maps generally would not show defective features such as ruined buildings, dung heaps or eyesores of any sort.

This point is made clear by comparison with Treswell's legal work. For instance, his map of Hailes Abbey mentioned above shows ruins above the manor house resulting from the Dissolution of the Monasteries, which would not appear on an estate map. What is shown supports the purpose of this map, made for a legal case to determine ownership and boundaries, including landmarks as they appeared at the time, since court officials might be walking the land. This contrasts with the purpose of the Dorset estate maps, which was to enable Hatton to feel pride as he viewed his estates from afar and to show them off to his friends, so ruins would not be included.

TNA MF 1/59 Treswell's map of Hailes Abbey

Specific areas of the maps merit comment, including use of scale, orientation, and style, and features depicted such as animals, topography and buildings.

SCALE AND LOCAL VARIATION

THE USE OF scale on maps in England dates to earlier in the 16th century, when it was first used by military engineers in the reign of Henry VIII, and so is associated with the importance of fortifications.[38]

Scale was a new feature when these maps were made, at a time when map literacy could not be assumed. Professional surveyors would take care to show that they had practised this new skill, and they might also explain how to read it. Dividers open above a scale bar point out the use of scale, and may literally point to a scale statement to show that an inch on the scale bar is measured to find out how many miles or perches that inch on the map represents on the ground.

The scale bar on the Isle of Purbeck map is in the lower left corner, surmounted by dividers and the words 'Scala Miliarium' meaning a scale in miles. This is the same placing and wording as the scale bar on the Saxton county map, which suggests that Treswell referred to it when making this map.[39]

Treswell returned to his usual style of scale bar for the other maps, signed and dated, with scale statements in English, about how many feet to a perch he had used. The perch was an old surveyor's measure which at this date could be found both as a standard length or statute perch of 16 and a half feet to a perch, and in local variations. The statute perch was the measure used by Hawsted for his map, and by Treswell for his both Northamptonshire and Dorset maps for Hatton.

On the five manor maps Treswell drew a second scale bar, for a customary perch of 15 feet 9 inches, which is presumably a local Dorset measure. It is unclear why Treswell used this second scale for these Dorset maps, when for the Northamptonshire and other maps he only drew one; perhaps he was assisted in measuring the land by local men, who used their usual measure. Local measures could vary considerably; the Devon customary measure was 18 feet to the perch.[40]

The maps vary from the smaller scale Purbeck overview map at 1 inch to about five-eighths of a mile, to the rather larger-scale manor maps at 1 inch to between about 40 and 55 perches, through to the Corfe Castle area map, drawn at a scale of 1 inch to 24 standard perches, or 25 customary perches. Presumably this was shown in greater detail, as it was the most important part of the estate. The ground plan of Corfe Castle used the smaller unit of feet rather than perches, to give a scale of one inch to 40 feet, a larger scale than the maps, to best show detail of the building.

ORIENTATION OF THE MAPS

RALPH TRESWELL MADE his maps with borders of two sets of double-ruled lines, in which he set the cardinal points in capital letters, in Latin, in the same way that Saxton had pioneered on his county maps.

At this date the convention of placing north at the top of a map had not yet emerged, although the Saxton county maps were all orientated to the north. Treswell's manuscript maps are oriented in different directions, presumably in order to best present irregularly shaped land parcels. Of his eight manuscript maps in this volume, three are orientated to the north and three to the east, while two have west at top. None are orientated to the south.[41] Hawsted's map of Corfe is oriented to the north, indicated not by written cardinal points, but by a large decorative compass rose with a north pointer marked N. The style and decoration are typical of early seventeenth century maps.

BUILDINGS ON THESE ESTATE MAPS

TRESWELL'S ESTATE MAPS and his earliest known plans of houses in London dated to 1585 were drawn using the contemporary technique of a bird's-eye view, where the buildings and landmark features such as hills and trees were drawn as pictures, as if viewed in perspective, at an angle, from above.[42]

The area map shows the towns of Wareham and Poole, outside the Isle of Purbeck, by drawings of houses clustered around the church. Within the Isle are the small towns of Corfe and Studland, with churches that may have been drawn from life, with grey stone roofs. Studland's church is drawn 'on its back' like many of the houses.

Villages are shown by text label [the name written as a word], and a church drawn above. Churches are drawn more or less the same as each other, like a conventional sign on a modern map, with the tower at left, usually with a door and two windows. Just one church, East Tyneham, has a spire.

Buildings, including Corfe Castle and borough on the manor map, are often drawn in rather odd perspective. The Castle seems partly drawn as if in bird's eye view, as seen from above, but the towers in the left hand curtain wall seem to lean in different directions, and the whole structure appears as if seen by someone standing at the church with their head turned to the left. Other buildings include the Parsonage to the west, drawn as a pictogram, like the other houses including those in Corfe borough. Other buildings shown include water mills; Arfleet Mill and West Mill are both drawn on the area map with their wheels in the river.

Detail of Corfe Castle

On all these maps, just a few houses either stand individually in the countryside or are grouped in hamlets, as at Newton Farm on the Newton manor map, presumably on the site of the failed medieval planned town of Newton. Houses are mainly drawn conventionally, as picture-symbols, with a door, two windows and often a chimney on each red-roofed house.

Treswell was careful to include the region's castles on the area map. Hatton as Admiral of Purbeck was responsible for the defence of the coast. He may have been aware of the coastal maps produced late in the reign of Henry VIII, when the break with Rome had then sparked defensive concerns and the production of a number of maps of the south coast of England, including Dorset.[43] While this is a landownership map, it was drawn at a time when Protestant England was aware of similar potential threats from Catholic Europe, especially from Spain and its feared Armada.

The most prominent building on Treswell's map is Corfe Castle, drawn in a rather strange perspective view, at this point shown still standing with curtain walls drawn to suggest their placement across the hill on which it stands. In Poole Harbour is the square tower of Brownsea ('Brucksey') Castle on Brownsea Island. Also shown is Studland Castle on Handfast Point from which it commanded views across two bays.

The individual Dorset manor maps show relatively few buildings. The area map shows Bindon Abbey in the west above Bindon Wood, in its post-Reformation guise as a manor house, with medieval towered gatehouse leading to a courtyard. Like Corfe Castle, also shown intact on these maps, it would be destroyed during the Civil War. The map gives us valuable images of places now much changed by history.

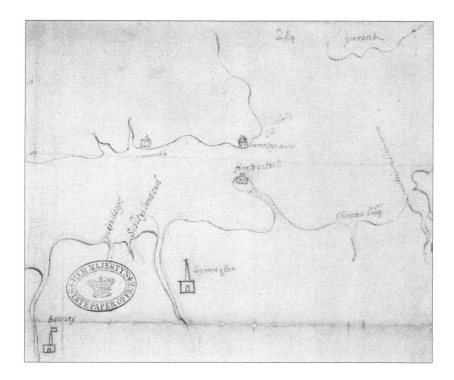

Part of coastal map dated 1587 from State Papers showing Purbeck at top right and the sea across to the Isle of Wight and Hurst Castle on the Hampshire coast (the map faces south). Notes on the map list landing places with numbers of men guarding them.
TNA MPF 1/135

TRESWELL'S CORFE CASTLE PLAN

THE EXCEPTION TO this style is the Corfe Castle plan in this volume. It is a ground plan, which may be because Treswell was aware that fortifications were generally drawn in this more advanced style. By the 1580s other building plans were often shown in ground plan, too, so Treswell may have become aware of this style because his patron, Hatton, and Hatton's colleagues such as Burghley, were building large houses, and indeed Treswell worked in them.

The castle is shown in plan, with the outer walls coloured grey, and interior spaces of the buildings coloured brown. Exterior spaces are uncoloured, and denoted by text label eg 'The Garden'. The large scale enabled Treswell to show details of bridges and gatehouses, steps, latrines, towers, windows, a stable (in the right hand wall of the outer ward), the 'steare leading up into ye kings Tower'. A gun platform with six cannon are the only details to be shown pictorially, which emphasises that the castle was an important fortress – as would be attested during the Civil War. Within the castle proper are noted the 'new bulwarke' with two cannon, courts, vaults, the Queen's Tower, the King's Tower, a garden and a well. Treswell included outworks, a ditch, and the castle mound which he called 'A Steepe hill of rock'.

This is the most substantial building known outside London to be drawn by Treswell, apart from the palatial Holdenby House which is shown pictorially in the wider landscape of the manor on Treswell's map for Hatton, and Esher Place, drawn by Treswell in 1606.[44]

Treswell appears not to have used the ground plan again to depict buildings, until he came to work on the sets of London house plans in the years 1607-12. His plan of Clothworkers' Hall in Mincing Lane exhibits similar depiction of staircases with hatching to suggest treads, privies and wells.[45] The use of ground plan could be seen as a step in the evolution of the plan style to which he would return decades later.

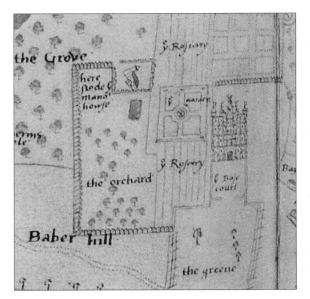 

Hatton's House at Holdenby, Northamptonshire Record Office reference:OLILC2HA (left). Part of map showing Esher Place, 1606, then owned by Francis Drake's family, by Ralph Treswell the Elder, TNA, MPEE 1/213 (right)

LANDSCAPE DEPICTION

THERE IS LITTLE to indicate the rise and fall of the land, but hills are drawn as rounded mounds, in the same way as on Saxton's map, with shading on the right hand side. These are rare features on the peninsula, apart from the Purbeck Ridge, and are often named. Three notable hills are ranged across Studland Heath: Ryecroft, Black Down and the Agglestone Rock with a large tor atop. On Bovington Heath to the west of the Isle map appear a group named 'The 5 barrowes'. Treswell had difficulty in depicting the prominent hilltop on which Corfe Castle sits, which appears flat on the area map. It is conveyed on the manor map by the legend 'Castle Hill', and shading around the castle. The town houses are angled to indicate that they are built on a slope; some aligned along the street while others are shown at right angles to it.

No roads were shown on Saxton's county maps nor on Treswell's overview map of the Isle of Purbeck, possibly to keep their style relatively uncluttered at this smaller scale. Treswell includes some roads on the larger scale maps, often shown crossing each other or bounding lands, and usually indicated by solid lines, while paths tend to be shown using double pecked lines. Sometimes the place to which the route leads is written. The road pattern in the towns of Corfe and Studland is also shown.

It was important that Treswell showed the outer boundaries of the manor, itself coloured green, so that ownership was clear, and potential disputes could be avoided. The overview map gives the boundary of the Isle of Purbeck, by a text note at top left, traced on the map as a 'perambulation' or circular mental trail around the route, with a start and end point at a way between Whiteway Hill and 'Flowerborrow' Hill' [Flowersbery in the text], an Iron Age fort high above Worbarrow Bay at lower left, the western point of the Purbeck Ridge. From thence the boundary is traced to Wareham, presumably along the rivers, and clockwise around the coast via St Aldhelm's Chapel. Rivers on boundaries are included, drawn as wavy lines, some coloured blue, usually not named. Beyond the bounds of Hatton's estate no detail is shown nor are these areas drawn to scale, but adjoining landowners are named.

Within each of Hatton's manors fields and their boundaries are carefully drawn, as land parcels apportioned to different tenants, who may be named. How the fields were cultivated affected their value, so the mapmaker indicates this, usually by text label as arable, pasture, and meadow. Some arable fields on the Studland and Corfe maps were cultivated in common, and are shown in strips, bundles of which run in different directions. Some signs of enclosure of common land appear; at the top of the Corfe Castle area map is a note 'Inclosed grounds to norden'. 'Newly Inclosed' land on the Middlebere Heath map show two fields recently fenced off from the heath.

Field furniture such as stiles and gates occur frequently on these maps, shown by picture symbols, where they occur on field boundaries or at the end of footpaths. Boundary stones and crosses on the manor boundaries are shown especially on the heathlands where no river or other boundary marker was evident. On the Middlebere Heath map is a mound surmounted by a structure marked 'the gallows'.

Treswell drew a fire beacon on the Langton Wallis map, on the northern (left) edge of Ailwood Down. This was important as part of the chain of warning beacons erected on heights at this time to be lit on view of the Armada, and also because good vantage points were important in survey work.

Other common landscape elements on the maps are individual trees and woods, shown by name - Bindon Wood and Lulworth Wood in the far west of the area map - or by clusters of trees. Norden Wood, north-east of the Castle on the Corfe map, has trees set out in a grid, as a plantation. An orchard and coppice are labelled on the Newton Heath map, which has a withy bed on the bay, and 'salts' bordering the sea, presumably the site of salt pans.[46] These also appear on the Middlebere map. East and West Salterne place names on the Studland map also suggest salt workings.

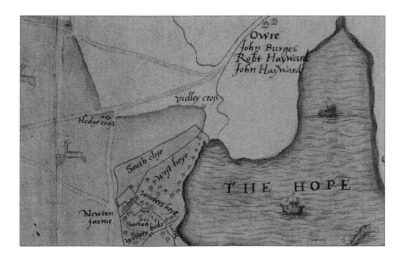

Treswell: section of the Newton Heath map showing withy beds and 'salts'.

The coast is drawn in some detail on several of these maps, as one might expect given Hatton's position as Admiral of the Isle of Purbeck. The overview map shows the creeks, bays and islands, and the narrow defended channel into Poole Harbour. The shape of the coastline shows much change in some places, such as the Studland map with the sweep of the Bay from South Haven peninsula facing Brownsea Island to Handfast Point (top right) with the Pinnacles and St Lucas Leap. The freshwater lagoon of Little Sea is shown with an open side onto the bay, before dunes developed.

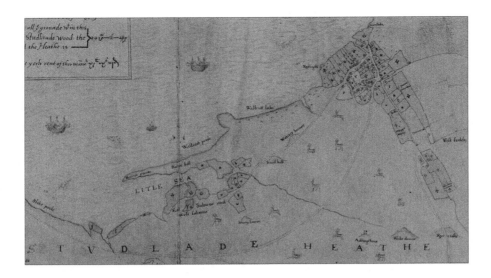

Treswell: section of the Studland map showing the Little Sea

In some cases there is place-name change, where the maps give old names such as 'The Hope' (now Newton Bay) on the Newton Heath map. The landscape term 'ord' seems to refer to a headland or spit. There are four named ords along the west coast of the South Haven peninsula adjoining Little Sea: Rickmans, Geries, Coke and Rede. Towards Handfast Point a headland bears the note 'the 3 ordes'

DECORATION

THE APPLICATION OF gold leaf to some of the maps on the dividers and on the initial capital letters of legends is a sign that they were intended to be prestigious artefacts for display.

Treswell: section of the key map of the Isle of Purbeck

A charming feature of these maps is the way Treswell included drawings of animals: deer and rabbits, swans, all valuable for their meat. These appear to be shown in areas where they actually ranged, and may reflect the fact that Hatton had the right to hunt red deer and the right to warren, since the manor he held was Crown property.[47] The animals serve a useful decorative function in providing interest in areas of heathland where there would otherwise be little detail shown. They are drawn larger than life, not to scale; on the Isle of Purbeck map, one of the deer is drawn five times larger than the cottage next to it.

The deer include stags with antlers and hinds without; leaping, standing, lying down, or with neck bent as if about to graze. Rabbits galore appear on the headland to the north of Middlebere Heath, 'the great pasture being full of furseys', where squiggles suggest the burrows of their warren. One rabbit is drawn jumping out of his hole.

Treswell: section of the Middlebere map showing the warren

Were these animals perhaps drawn from a pattern book? There is a similarity with rabbits drawn by John Lane on his 1580 map of Methwold Warren in Norfolk, although his rabbits are shown in silhouette. In the inner most bay of Poole Harbour a flock of fifteen swans is drawn, all facing towards the land. This was one of a number of swanneries in the area at this time. They look similar to those on a 1571 map of Sturmer Mere in Essex and one on the Hailes Abbey map.[48]

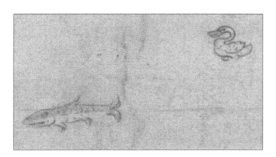

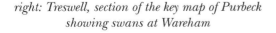

above: Images of a swan and a fish from Sturmer Mere map, TNA: MPC 1/33.

right: Treswell, section of the key map of Purbeck showing swans at Wareham

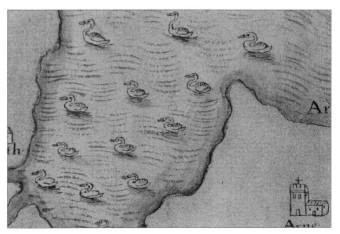

The sea is full of interest. Fish often appear; some may indicate areas of fishing where smaller boats are also shown, while others appear to be catfish or more akin to sea monsters, as on the Newton Heath map. The three-masted ships may be a reference to the defensive position of the Isle of Purbeck in relation to the coast of France, or to the pirates which are known to have plagued these shores in these decades.

Human figures are rarely shown on early maps, but three are drawn on the Middlebere map as silhouettes like the Methwold rabbits, each with hat, jacket, breeches and long staff; two on the heath carry furze-cutters, and one on the headland represents a warrener or rabbit-farmer. People appear more plentifully on the Northamptonshire maps Treswell made for Hatton, on three of eight maps. This may be because the Dorset maps mainly show a sparsely populated heathland landscape, compared to the pastoral Midland countryside. Treswell may have put more decoration on the Midlands maps because they show Hatton's main estates.

JOHN HAWSTED'S MAP OF CORFE MANOR

THIS ONLY MANUSCRIPT map in the volume by a mapmaker other than Ralph Treswell is by John Hawsted or Hausted: at the lower edge in capital letters is the name 'JOHN HAWSTEED'. This is likely to be the surveyor of that name who apparently made a map in 1610 of Geddington in Northamptonshire, alongside the mapmaker Thomas Thorpe.[49]

Thomas was one of the Thorpe family of masons and architects from Kingscliffe; his father was mason or architect to Hatton at Kirby Hall.[50] Hawsted may have got the commission for the Corfe map through his connection with the Thorpes, who had worked for Hatton. A further connection was that Thomas's more famous brother was the architect John Thorpe, who from 1611 was assistant to Ralph's son Robert Treswell, Surveyor-General of Woods South of the Trent.

The first map attributed to Hawsted alone is dated 1616.[51] He is known to have worked in Northamptonshire and surrounding counties; this map adds Dorset to the compass of his work.[52] There are few other dates for Hawsted, and since his Corfe map is undated, it was presumably made between 1610, when Hawsted is first mentioned as a surveyor, and the destruction of Corfe Castle during the Civil War, in 1646, since it is shown intact on Hawsted's map. A closer dating for the map of 1610-1620 is provided by conservation work on the binding of the volume which suggests that it was bound in its present order including this map, no later than 1620.

Treswell had earlier made a map of the Corfe area, so why include in the volume this later map, probably dating from the second decade of the seventeenth century? This map shows lands extending to the north of Corfe Castle, which belonged to the Daccombe family, and features relating to the borders of the two estates that had been omitted by Treswell. To accommodate the extra area this map is at a slightly larger scale of 1 inch to 20 perches, compared with Treswell's at 1 inch to 24 perches.

Comparison of the two maps where they show the same lands around the castle allows us to see any changes. Hawsted writes the acreage across each named field in the form of three numbers: the first representing the number of acres, then the rods, and perches. These were important facts for estate management. They were traditionally supplied by the surveyor as part of written text; but it was very useful to have the figures on the actual plot, to gain a visual grasp of size of land parcels.

CONCLUSION

THESE MAPS WERE a product of a specific need for Hatton at a time when mapmaking was beginning to flourish. If their initial purpose was to give their owner prestige and a view of his estates, their legacy is an important cache of the earliest known estate maps for Dorset.

These maps are good examples of exciting new developments in the 1580s, with the emergence of the estate map as a genre and of professional surveyors such as Treswell. Together with the maps of Hatton's Northamptonshire lands, this is a substantial corpus which contributes to our understanding of Elizabethan cartography.

These maps are an attractive and detailed depiction of these places in early modern times, as seen by a contemporary mapmaker. There is much that is pictorial, which engages our imagination and means we can readily identify houses and trees, while taking in a wider view. Historic maps such as these are an immediate way for us to see over centuries both continuity and change in the landscape.

1   The political background to the rise in map consciousness is considered in an overview of mapmaking in England, ca.1550-1611 Barber, P. *Cartography in the European Renaissance*, volume 3 part 2 of the *History of Cartography*, 2007, University of Chicago Press, pp. 1608-1620.

2   Burghley's use of maps is recorded in many sources including a section on 'Lord Burghley, maps, and government' pp. 68-77 in Barber, P. 'England II: Monarchs, Ministers and Maps, 1550-1625' in Buisseret, D., ed., *Monarchs, Ministers and Maps*, 1992, University of Chicago Press, pp. 57-98. A study of maps drawn by Burghley appears in Margey, A. and Andrews, J. H. 'A Hitherto Unknown Sketch Map by Lord Burghley', *Imago Mundi*, 2012, vol. 64, pp. 96-100; a sketch map of Liddesdale is reproduced in P. D. A. Harvey, *Maps in Tudor England*, British Library and Public Record Office, London, 1993, plate 34, p. 53.

3   Burghley's letter is cited in Beresford, M. *History on the Ground*, London, Methuen, 1971, pp.210-211, where it is noted that a measure of the speed of change in the landscape was that Saxton's map of Northamptonshire was published four years before Hatton started to build his house at Holdenby.

4   Vines, A. G. *Neither Fire nor Steel: Sir Christopher Hatton*, Chicago, Nelson-Hall, 1978, p.125.

5   Bendall, S. *Maps, Land and Society: A History, with a Carto-bibliography of Cambridgeshire Estate Maps, c. 1600–1836*, Cambridge University Press, 1992, especially sections on the surveying profession in early modern England, pp. 77-80, and surveying techniques, pp.129-38.

6   Evans I. and Lawrence, H. *Christopher Saxton, Elizabethan Map-Maker*, Wakefield Historical Publications and The Holland Press, 1979, chap. 8; Bower, D. 'Saxton Manuscript Maps and Surveys Not Described by Evans and Lawrence', *Imago Mundi*, 2010, vol. 62 pt 2, pp.191-204; Shannon, W. 'Christopher Saxton's Last Maps: Nichol Forest and the Debateable Land, 1607', *Imago Mundi*, 2016, vol. 68 pt 1, pp.1-15; Beresford *History on the Ground*, pp.52-62.

7   Barber, 'England II: Monarchs, Ministers and Maps', Dorset map notes p.74.

8   Techniques and surveyors' texts are discussed Evans and Lawrence *Christopher Saxton, Elizabethan Map-maker*, pp. 40-44.

9   Evans and Lawrence *Christopher Saxton, Elizabethan Map-Maker*, analysis of the supposed sequence in which maps were made, p.12, presents arguments for and against a suggested westward progress of the survey.

10 Evans and Lawrence *Christopher Saxton, Elizabethan Map-Maker*, provide a table with the different scales of all the county maps, p.39.

11 Evans and Lawrence *Christopher Saxton, Elizabethan Map-Maker*, note that Seckford changed this motto sometime during 1576, p.11.

12 Harvey, P. D. A. 'An Elizabethan map of manors in North Dorset', in *British Museum Quarterly*, (1965) vol. 29, pp 82-84, the Queen had granted Purse Caundle to Hatton in 1569-1570. Part of the map is illustrated in colour as plate 77 in Tyacke S. and Huddy, J. *Christopher Saxton and Tudor map-making*, The British Library, 1980. Barker suggests that the map was made to show lands of the Bishop of Salisbury, 'Elizabethan Map of North-west Dorset' in Barker K. and Kain, R. J. P. eds, *Maps and History in South-West England*, University of Exeter Press, 1991.

13 Harvey, P. D. A. 'English Estate Maps: their early history and their use as historical evidence', in Buisseret, D., ed., *Rural Images: estate maps in the Old and New Worlds*, University of Chicago Press, 1996, pp. 27-61; p. 27 lists early estate maps. Also in Harvey, P. D. A. *Manors and Maps in Rural England*, Ashgate Variorum Collected Studies Series, 2010, section XVII.

14 Ravenhill M. and Rowe M., eds., *Devon Maps and Map-makers: Manuscript Maps before 1840*, Devon and Cornwall Record Society, New Series, vol. 43, 2000 (companion vol. 45 published 2002) pp. 5 and 67. A sketch map of lands near Axminster, part of Devon estates of the late Duke of Norfolk, dated 1574, is the earliest Devon map to state a scale. The mapmaker may be Sir Barnard or Bernard Drake, another of Elizabeth I's courtiers and an

explorer who accompanied Raleigh in setting up the first English colony in America, Roanoke. He may have been related to Francis Drake.

15 Harvey 'English Estate Maps', p. 27.

16 Reproduced in colour as plate 58 in Harvey, *Maps in Tudor England* and in black and white in Harvey, 'English Estate Maps' p. 28.

17 Reproduced in colour as plate 59 in Harvey, *Maps in Tudor England*.

18 Bendall *Maps, Land and Society*, p. 25.

19 Listed in detail including dates and dimensions of maps, in Schofield, J. *The London surveys of Ralph Treswell*, London Topographical Society Publication no. 135, 1987.

20 Beresford *History on the Ground*, discussed p.154, part of map reproduced as plate 14.

21 Eden, P. 'Three Elizabethan estate surveyors' in Tyacke, S., ed., *English Map-making 1500-1650*, London, British Library, 1983, pp. 70-72 and title cartouche illustrated as plate 33.

22 Barber, P. 'John Darby's Map of the Parish of Smallburgh in Norfolk, 1582', in *Imago Mundi* vol. 57 (2005), pp. 55-58 and illustrated in colour as plate 6.

23 Partially reproduced in colour Palmer, J. *Three Tudor Surveys*, Dorset Record Society, 2015, vol. 18, p.59.

24 Schofield *The London surveys of Ralph Treswell*.

25 Gerhold, D. *London Plotted: plans of London Buildings c.1450-1720*, London Topographical Society publication no. 178, 2016, p. 10.

26 The quote and this possibility is mentioned in Gerhold, D. 'New light on Ralph Treswell senior and junior', in *London Topographical Record*, vol. 31, 2015, pp. 45-49.

27 Treswell dated four of the Dorset maps: one to 1585 (the map of lands around Corfe Castle) and three to 1586 (the Corfe Castle plan, and maps of Studland and Langton Wallis). The maps of the Isle of Purbeck and Middlebury are undated. The date on the Newton Heath map is incomplete; it may have been made at the end of one year, and its completion date was uncertain.

28 For dating see Schofield *The London surveys of Ralph Treswell*, p. 5 which shows a table of map dates derived from the work of Ralph Hyde. For an examination of the pre- and post- enclosure map evidence at Holdenby, see Beresford *History on the Ground*, pp. 212-213.

29 Schofield *The London surveys of Ralph Treswell*, p. 1.

30 Map of St Martins and St Giles, The National Archives, reference: MPB 1/1 extracted from E 178/1391. Map of Hailes Abbey: The National Archives, reference: MF 1/59 extracted from court proceedings at E 178/910. It's significance as a legal map is discussed in 'Maps in Sixteenth-Century English Law Courts', R. Mitchell, *Imago Mundi*, vol. 58 (2006), pp. 212-8; for an archaeological examination of the map see Brown, G. *English Heritage Research Department report 29*, 2006. Map of Esher, Surrey: The National Archives, reference: MPEE 1/213 formerly LRRO 1/2765.

31 Schofield *The London surveys of Ralph Treswell*, plates 1 and 2 for the early plans.

32 Schofield *The London surveys of Ralph Treswell*, page 3 and details of all Treswell's known surveys at date of publication in table, p. 6; a supplementary list is on p. 48 of Gerhold, 'New light on Ralph Treswell'; the manor of Candover map of 1588 illustrated in black and white as Figure 2.6 in *Rural Images: estate maps in the old and new worlds*, page 34 (caption apparently transposed with that of Figure 2.5).

33 Bendall *Maps, Land and Society*, p. 94.

34 Two coloured areas at left of the Isle of Purbeck map have no such maps.

35 Saxton's map of Sittingbourne, Kent, 1590, partly reproduced as plate 64 in Harvey *Maps in Tudor England*, with very similar compass indicator and cardinal points.

36 The National Archives, reference: MPC 1/75; illustrated in colour and described in Mitchell R. and Janes, A. *Maps: their untold stories; map treasures from The National Archives*, Bloomsbury, 2014, pp. 40-41.

37 Illustrated in 'The map collection of William Cecil, first Baron Burghley, 1520-1598', Harley, J. B. *The Map Collector*, Issue 3, 1978, p.13.

38 Harvey, P. D. A. 'Estate surveyors and the spread of the scale map in England 1550-80', *Landscape History*, 1993, vol. 15, pp. 37-49.

39 Measuring the map gives a scale of two inches to one and a quarter miles [8 inches to 5 miles] or 1 inch to about five-eighths of a mile.

40 Ravenhill and Rowe *Devon maps and map makers*, p. 5.

41 The three Treswell maps oriented to the north are that of the Isle of Purbeck; Treswell's plan of Corfe Castle and his Corfe manor map. Hawsted's map of Corfe also has north at top of the map, making four maps to the north. The three maps oriented to the east are Studland Heath, the Langton area and Langton parcel maps. Two maps are oriented to the west: Newton Heath and Middlebere.

42 In Tothill Street and Cheapside, Schofield, *The London surveys of Ralph Treswell*, plates 1 and 2.

43 *Cartography in the European Renaissance, volume 3 part 2*, p. 1604 includes mention of a map of the Dorset coast from Poole to Lyme (part of which is illustrated in *Maps in Tudor England* plate 26), and a chart of Poole harbour, both cited in footnote 115.

44 Northamptonshire Record Office reference:OLILC2HA. Part of map showing Esher Place,1606, then owned by Francis Drake's family, by Ralph Treswell the Elder, The National Archives, reference: MPEE 1/213

45 Schofield *The London surveys of Ralph Treswell*, plate 4.

46 There were 32 salterns or salt pans on the southern shores of Poole Harbour in the time of Domesday, according to Beaton, D. *Dorset Maps*, Dovecote Press, 2001, p. 15. The term 'salter' can also refer to a deer-leap, stile or place where deer could enter a park; there are deer shown on this map, but since they do not appear to be emparked, the salt association is clear here. Cooper G. J. and Shannon, W. D. 'The control of salters (deer-leaps) in private deer-parks associated with forests: a case study using a 1608 map of Leagram park in the Forest of Bowland, Lancashire' in *Landscape History*, 2017, vol. 38, especially p. 45. For more on the contemporary salt industry see Higham, M. C. 'Take it with a pinch of salt', *Landscape History*, 2003, vol. 25, pp. 59-65.

47 Brooks, E. St John, *Sir Christopher Hatton, Queen Elizabeth's Favourite*, Jonathan Cape, 1947, p. 112.

48 The National Archives, reference: MPC 1/33, reproduced in Mitchell and Janes *Maps: their untold stories*, pp.36-37.

49 The National Archives, reference: MPBB 1/2/1 Plan showing the line of procession of Geddington, Northamptonshire, drawn by Thomas Thorpe and John Hawsted, surveyors, 1610. Map with legal depositions taken 27 September 1610 in a boundary dispute, where John Hausteed is noted as a gentleman of Oundle, Northamptonshire, aged 29; The National Archives, reference: E 178/4318 membrane 4.

50 Summerson, J. *Architecture in Britain 1530 to 1830*, Penguin,1953, p. 38; John Thorpe stated that he laid the first stone of Kirby Hall in 1570, when he was a child, which suggests that his father Thomas Thorpe (d.1596) was the principal mason of the building. J. Summerson 'John Thorpe and the Thorpes of Kingscliffe', *Architectural Review*, 1949, pp.291-300.

51 M. Beresford notes John Hawsted as having made a map of Pickwell in 1616, in 'Glebe terriers and open-field Leicestershire', in *Studies in Leicestershire Agrarian History*, Hoskins, W. G., ed., Leicestershire Archaeological Society, 1949, pp.77-126.

52 Bendall, S. A., ed., *Dictionary of land surveyors and local map-makers of Great Britain and Ireland 1530-1850*, 2nd edition, British Library, 1997, entry H204 notes Hawsted's work also in Huntingdonshire, Leicestershire and Lincolnshire.

THE CONDITION AND CONSERVATION OF THE MAPS AND SURVEY

When examining a manuscript volume it is not only the written content that reveals the history of the document. The binding of a book can provide much fascinating information and the Treswell Survey is a perfect example of this.

Historically, books were not bought ready-bound. Loose sheets were transported, bought and sold, and were only covered at the owners behest. A volume was bound as a unique object at a binder's workshop, often far, both in time and geographically, from where the text was produced. Therefore the date of creation of a text can rarely be relied upon to date its binding. The style of binding, ranging from temporary paper covers to full leather with gold decoration and metal furniture, reflected the taste and wealth of the owner as well as the value they placed upon the text. Beyond the external features of a volume, the paper, sewing, endbands and boards, can all provide evidence of a bindings use and importance, and these too can be explored within the Treswell Survey.

MATERIALS AND CONSTRUCTION

Paper

The Treswell Survey was created in a period significant in the history of paper production in England. Paper, widely considered to be invented in China around 100 BC, made slow progress across the world to Europe. The first paper mill in England was established in 1494 but only remained in production for four years due to strong competition from more established European mills.[1] After the closure of this mill, paper production in England did not resume as a significant industry until the late seventeenth century.[2] As such it is likely that the Treswell Survey was produced upon paper imported from Europe.

Interestingly, at first glance the written survey and the maps created by Treswell appear to be from the same paper stock, comparing their colour, weight and texture. Upon examination there are in fact fifteen different watermarks, and as each watermark can largely be attributed to an individual paper mill, this would seem to be an unexpected discovery. However, this is not uncommon in historic books and many volumes of this age are found to have paper stock from various mills, though the reason for this is still speculative.[3] By the time of the Treswell Survey's creation there were thousands of watermark designs, representing animals, vegetation or even the name of a mill and date of production. They cannot be relied upon to place or date a paper source as designs were often copied from one mill to another.

Within the written survey, there are eight different watermarks, which appear alternatingly throughout the textblock, suggesting the papers were bought together, rather than a limited amount was bought from one mill, expended and then the next stock bought. Some of the paper used for the maps match those within the survey, for example, the Purbeck map, Corfe map and page 48 in the written survey are the same paper. The use of the same paper within the written survey and the maps implies that they were created at the same time.

Saxton's and Hawsted's maps and the contents page are noticeably different paper stock, in colour and weight, to the Treswell Survey and are clearly separate additions to the volume.

Watermark Page 48

Inks

THE SURVEY IS written in iron gall ink, as are occasional annotations on the maps. This ink was usually made by the writer and there are various historical recipes, resulting in non-standardised ink comprising of numerous ingredients. The Treswell and Hawsteed maps have also been drawn in this type of ink and completed with watercolour. Saxton's map of Dorsetshire was printed from engraved copper plates before being coloured by hand. Additional gold pigment has been used on some maps to highlight features such as dividers, capital letters and deer, the latter a nod to Hatton's Golden Hind crest.

Golden hind Isle of Purbeck Map

There is a form of pagination in iron gall ink at the top right corner throughout the textblock. This numbering is not consistent, with numbers being allocated to the recto of every leaf, whilst assigned intermittently to the verso. They are likely to have been used to ensure the preferred order before binding and were written prior to the textblock being 'ploughed' or trimmed, to create flush edges after sewing, as seen on the Langton Wallis map.

Trimmed number Langton Matravers Map

Construction

WHEN A VOLUME has undergone repair, there are often remnants from the original binding that provide evidence of the book's initial construction. Protrusions on the inside of the paste boards (boards constructed from layers of compressed paper, which predominantly replaced wooden boards at this time) suggest the text block was originally sewn onto five cords which were laced in to the boards. However there are no remains of the original sewing thread or endbands. It is likely the volume would have had hand-sewn endbands, probably of two colour threads, but damage to the folds of the sections has removed any evidence of holes that might be associated with hand-sewn endbands. Similarly the original endpapers have been replaced and no evidence remains of their composition, although at this period they may have been a simple construction of plain paper or waste vellum.

Leather/tooling

BINDING DESIGNS CHANGED continually over time and so it is possible to date a volume by the decoration used. Due to recognisable periods of fashion, it is possible to date the Treswell binding to the late sixteenth or early seventeenth century, contemporary with the production of the survey. This is evidenced by the gold tooling centrepiece and corner fleurons on the front board, which are typical of the style favoured in Elizabethan England c.1580-1620.[4] It is possible the original spine had received some decoration around the raised bands, although there is no remaining evidence. Whilst not being the most elaborate of designs, the fashionable tooling would indicate to anyone visiting Hatton that this volume was of some importance.

left: Centrepiece ; right: fleuron

Repairs and new material

BOOKS ARE MECHANICAL objects and the joints of a binding, where the boards meet the spine, receive the most wear due to the stress exerted upon them every time the volume is opened. Rebacks, where the spine is removed and new material is used to repair the broken joints, are not unusual. This treatment was often accompanied by replacing the endpapers, repair of the textblock and re-sewing if necessary.

This work has been carried out on the Treswell Survey, evidenced at first glance by the new leather covering the spine. Examining the volume it was possible to see that during the reback the original thread was removed and the textblock was resewn. Substantial damage had occurred to the folds of the sections which meant the repairing binder was unable to resew the textblock in the traditional fashion. To overcome this, they whip-stitched the sections (where thread is passed through the side of a collection of leaves and brought round the back, rather than through a central fold) and used this to support each section before sewing them all back together.

Whip-stitching

During the reback, the maps received significant repair work. Each bifolio, the single sheet of paper folded to make two leaves, was lined with paper on the verso, and a cloth joint was adhered to the fold. This process of lining was not always successful and there are areas of tension and bubbling. Additional paper repairs and infills were added to the edges of the majority of the maps, and in some places these obscure text and image. However, the addition of the cloth joint did provide a layer of support to the weakened paper and prevented further damage occurring to the maps when they were resewn.

Machine-made endbands of red and gold were adhered at each end of the spine, and new endpapers consisting of a pasted-down bifolio and two additional flyleaves were added. The leather reback has a hollow spine with seven false raised bands to imitate sewing cords beneath the leather, a method of suggesting the sewing structure was more substantial than that executed.

It is possible to estimate a date of these repairs from the materials and actions used by the repairer. When the pastedown of the new endpapers was adhered to the front board a window was cut to accommodate the inscription. The latest of these annotations was dated to 1835, indicating that the new pastedowns would have been attached after this date. However, it is the addition of the machine-made endbands that provide the earliest possible date of repair as these were only patented in 1851, before which endbands were sewn by hand.[5]

The volume has undergone at least one further restoration since the 1850s, when leather repairs were carried out to the corners and edges of the board. Differing leather implies either two separate repair events, or that small pieces of scrap leather were used during one occasion and the repairer was indifferent to the mismatch.

CONSERVATION

THE PREDOMINANT ISSUE for the preservation and study of this volume was the tight whip-stitched sewing. This prevented it from opening flat and obscured the section of the image contained in the central fold of the maps.

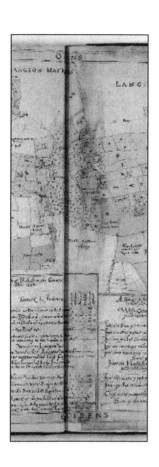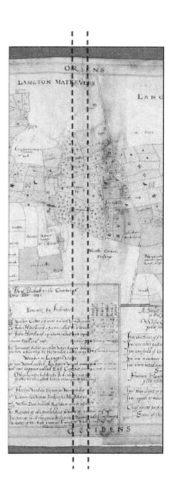

Obscured detail in central fold before and after disbinding

To reveal this hidden section the volume was disbound. This course of action was deemed appropriate as it released the concealed part of the image for research purposes and allowed digitisation; providing greater access to a wider audience. It also ensured future preservation by limiting the need to access the original. All evidential material was retained for future examination.

The leather binding was removed from the paper textblock by carefully cutting down the endpaper joints. The textblock was held vertically in a laying press and a poultice of methylcellulose was applied to the spine. This gel-like substance softens the animal glue which was used to adhere the spine linings, allowing it to be gently scraped away without risk of wetting the paper of the text-block. Removal of the spine linings provided access to the sewing, which was carefully cut and the sections separated. The whip-stitching was released from the survey sections to prevent any further tension from the thread potentially damaging the paper.

The binding and textblock were cleaned using a soft goat hair brush and a latex sponge was used to remove heavier deposits of surface dirt. An accumulation of dirt in the fold of the maps was mechanically removed using a micro-spatula.

The historic paper repairs carried out to the maps were not removed as, whilst they are not sympathetic to the original, they do not create detrimental tensions to the paper and are part of its historic context.

The flattened maps were each placed within a folded sheet of archival paper to protect the gold pigment from abrasion. These, the written survey and the original binding were then placed within their own four-flap folder made from archival board. A clear polyester pocket containing a sample of the sewing threads, cords and machine-made endbands was stored in the folder with the original binding. A bespoke adhesive-free archival clamshell box was created to house the three folders and a comprehensive post-treatment report provides future researchers and conservators with a record of the binding structure and work carried out.

The Treswell Survey as a material entity provides evidence which allows us to date its construction, identify the process behind its compilation and to understand its use through history. Its continued importance, by providing evidence in legal cases centuries after its creation, warranted the investment in its repair and restoration. The lifespan of this volume provides an appeal for the modern historian as captivating as its production did for viewers five centuries ago.

1   The first paper mill in England was John Tate's mill in Hertfordshire, Hunter, D. *Papermaking: History and Technique of an Ancient Craft.* Dover, 1978, p. 116.

2   Middleton, B. *A History of English Craft Bookbinding Technique,* London, 1978, p. 3.

3   Hunter, *Papermaking: History and Technique,* p. 261.

4   Pearson, D. *English Bookbinding Styles 1450-1800,* London, 2005, pp. 55, 126, 130.

5   *Official Catalogue of the Great Exhibition of the Works of Industry of All Nations 1851* reprinted Cambridge University Press, 2011.

THE CONTEXT OF THE WRITTEN SURVEY

WRITTEN TUDOR SURVEYS generally followed the instructions set out in contemporary manuals for estate stewards.[1] They include descriptions of lands, and notes about the different classifications of tenants, terms of tenure, monetary rents, rents in kind and the customs of the manor. Most surveys were conservative documents, recording those rights, customs, responsibilities and tenures that were in everyday use as well as those that were hazily remembered and destined to become obsolete. Occasionally they might record recent changes such as the enclosures at Okeford Fitzpaine recorded by the surveyor Richard Wright in 1586.[2]

The survey compiled to accompany Ralph Trewell's map contains the information required by the lord and his steward to maximise profits on the estate as it existed, without any modification or restructure, and to recognise any legal rights or restrictions. It asks the fundamental questions: who holds each property? What land does each property contain? By what right and on what terms do the tenants hold their land? What rents or services are payable upon it? What obligations does the lord have to the tenant? What rights does the lord have within his lands? The survey determined the value of the property and clarified the relationship between the lord and his tenants.

Compiling a survey was an expensive process so they were produced occasionally, perhaps once in each generation, often when a new lord acquired an estate. Ralph Treswell's written survey of Sir Christopher Hatton's land in Purbeck was compiled in 1586, to accompany his maps, once Hatton had completed his acquisitions in Dorset. It follows the standard formulae although, perhaps with his cartographic eye, it is set out more clearly than most and what he produced was by contemporary standards both expensive and extravagant: designed for display as much as for reference. An earlier survey for Langton Wallis, held in the Middleton Collection at Nottingham Univrsity Library, was compiled in 1546 and has a similar arrangement to Treswell's written survey.[3]

Beyond the rights to lands and rents, Treswell's survey is a compendium containing maps and surveys of manors, lands, a plan of the castle, an exemplification of Elizabeth I's charter grant to Hatton, the customs of the manors and of Corfe Castle borough and the rights of the Admiral of Purbeck. Sir Christopher Hatton had in a single document a work of reference that summarised all of his steward's rentals, court rolls, charters, agreements and custumals. These documents were kept in the estate muniment room which would have been packed with all of the evidences and ancient reference material that might be called upon to demonstrate the legal claims that are set out within the survey. With so many aspects of the estate summarised within a single document there is a large range of terms that often derive from medieval tenancies, local agricultural conditions and administrative areas that had developed over centuries. This section explains some of those terms and sets the survey within its Tudor context.

LAND AND TENANTS

THE TENANTS WHO occupied lands in Sir Christopher Hatton's estates held their land through a variety of tenancies that had developed over many centuries.

Freeholders held land that was nominally a part of the manor or estate and owed very minor rents and services. They usually paid a very low fixed rent or a rent in kind, such as a pound weight of wax, twenty horseshoes or a plough share. These rents had been fixed hundreds of years earlier so they were were of relatively low value by the end of the sixteenth century. Freeholders paid a *relief* on gaining inheritance to a property and, as this too was often fixed, the lord had little opportunity to realise a market value from freehold land. Some outlying lands, such as those at Eastington, Kimmeridge, Smedmore and Alfrington, were held by *knight's service* or *knight's fee*, a form of freehold that originally obliged the holder to provide a knight equipped for the military service, but by the sixteenth century had been commuted to a small annual rent.

Freeholders such as William Daccombe and Henry Uvedale were members of the gentry and manorial lords in their own right. There was no social stigma attached to holding property within another lord's manor; it was simply a method of increasing one's holdings, sometimes to increase a particular type of land such as a wood or meadow, or by acquiring a large block of property which could be leased to a farmer.

Corfe Castle was a borough with a charter which granted its inhabitants various rights and privileges. They held their properties or *burgages* freely and also had rights to participate in governing the borough. The burgages, inhabited by *burgesses,* were substantial dwellings with frontages along the main streets of the town with long plots running back to the arable fields.

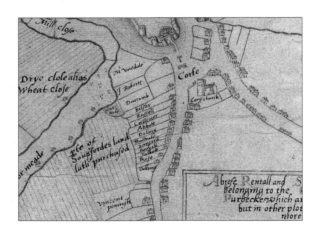

Detail of Corfe Castle burgages.

Although Hatton was lord of the manor of Corfe Castle and Keeper of the Castle itself he did not own all of the properties in the borough. However it is not possible to determine which were part of his estate. The names Cullener, Kilsby and Talbot appear beside burgage plots on the map, but they are not in the survey, while Welles, Atye, Tye and Perminter are in the survey, but not on the map. Several burgesses in the written survey held more than one property: Henry Bonvile had a shop and three burgages, John Barron had 'certain lands and burgages'. It seems unlikely that the map is incomplete or that the detail of landholding in Corfe Castle was too trivial to be fully documented. Perhaps Treswell originally conceived a detailed large scale map of the centre of the borough, like the map of the castle, which was not produced or has not survived.

The status of a tenant and the status of the land that they held is often expressed in the terminology of the courts through which these tenures were administered. The lord of a manor was always entitled to hold a *court baron*. This was an estate court, belonging to the lord, which tenants who owed services were obliged to attend. It was this right of the lord to hold a *court baron* that defined the manor as a *manor*. It was at this court that property was transferred, inheritances recorded and the terms of land holding established.

Most tenants held their land according to the *customs of the manor*. Consequently they were known as *customary* tenants or *copyholders* because they received a parchment copy of the entry in the proceedings of the manor court, the *court baron*, at which the terms and conditions of their tenancy were set out. They were the successors of the *villeins*, medieval peasants who had gained personal freedom in the fourteenth and fifteenth centuries, and were no longer considered to be chattels of the lord of the manor. The rights set out in these court rolls included rights for women to occupy land in widowhood, such as Edith Cotton and Edith Wylshere at Studland, or rights for land to descend through a family line when a widow remarried and to provide security for daughters by naming them in the agreement: William Mose, also of Studland, had a copyhold for the term of his life and those of Joan his wife and Margery their daughter successively.

The copyholders at Corfe Castle, Langton Wallis and Studland paid a fixed rent: William Mose of Studland paid 4s. 4d. for eight acres of arable, four acres of enclosed pasture and the right to put forty sheep on the common pasture of the chalk downs. Instead of a fixed relief the copyholders paid a variable *entry fine*, on 'entering' or taking up property, which was set by the lord and usually amounted to over ten year's rent, William Mose had paid £30, perhaps in several instalments. Thus the lord made the greater part of his income from copyholders when they inherited or took on new properties, from the fine that he set, rather than the ancient rent. They also paid a death duty from the property of the out-going tenant known as a *heriot*, which was traditionally their best animal, but could be commuted for a monetary payment. Additionally, the lord made an income by adding to the tenancy: copyhold was usually held for a term of lives and the incumbent tenant could pay a substantial fee to add extra lives to the agreement. By this means the tenants could achieve additional security for their families by adding the lives of younger people, usually their children, which could be expected to extend the terms of the lease.[4]

Freehold and copyhold land that came back into the hands of the lord for want of heirs was available for the lord to dispose of as he wished. Usually fresh agreements were made with new freehold or customary tenants on the same terms and conditions. But by the sixteenth century a third option, which was more attractive to landlords, was becoming more common: *leasehold*. By leasing property the lord had the opportunity to renegotiate the annual rent at the end of the term which enabled him to realise the current market value of the land and to have access to a predictable annual income that reflected the current value of the land.

Leasehold provided opportunities to merchants from towns, such as John Havellande of Poole, who invested in property for security, to have capital assets to borrow against and to advance their own families' ambitions to ascend to the gentry. John Havellande held a lease of the former site of Wilkeswood Priory with all its lands and buildings for the term of his own life and the life of his son Thomas. Leasehold removed the need to regulate customary tenants through a manor court and allowed the lord of the manor to dispense with the costs of administration. The manors of Afflington and Eastington provided significant revenues: £35 1s. 9d. and £74 1s. respectively, but as they were held by leasehold agreements they required very little management and do not have their own maps in the survey, although they feature on the key map. The rents from Studand and Langton Wallis, which have maps and detailed written sections, were £11 9s. 4d. and £86 6s.

The descriptions of lands vary depending upon the level of administration that they required. The steward might have to resolve disputes relating to the lands of the copyholders, so they have detailed listings of each close and the acrages that they held in the common fields. The freehold lands were not subject to the same scrutiny so, although in some cases they were quite valuable, they are often described only as 'certain lands and tenements'. John Clavell's knight's fees at Afflington, Little Kimmeridge, Smedmore and Langton were collectively worth £1 5s.

annually, but Treswell does not record their acreage. The leasehold lands were not administered through the court baron as intensively as the copyhold lands, but they required periodic renewal and are listed with the same degree of detail.

Freehold, burgage, copyhold and leasehold were the methods of landholding on Hatton's estates and the form of landholding is stated for each property. But, there were also outlying lands, which owed rents to support the Castle, where the conditions by which they were held are not stated. Lands in and around Wareham were worth almost £10 annually, but there are no details of their tenures and the acreages were added to the margin as an after thought.

CUSTOMS

THE CUSTOMS OF the lord and tenants within the written survey represent two aspects of the Purbeck estate. Firstly, customary payments which derived from a time when coins were not readily available and essential items were supplied as rent instead as a payment in kind. These include the pound of wax paid by William Daccombe or twenty horseshoes paid by Henry Uvedale. From the thirteenth century these items were often commuted to a monetary payment set at a fixed sum to ensure that goods of a certain standard were supplied. However, by the late sixteenth century when Treswell compiled his survey the assessments of the payments in kind were far lower than the contemporary value and the freeholders had the advantage in the deal. Copyholders also made customary payments in kind such as a bushels of wheat owed by the tenants of the tithings of Langton Wallis, Lutton and Worth, although most of these had also been changed to monetary payments.

Secondly, customs defined the rights and responsibilities of the lord and his tenants. The lord could lay claim to the cargo of wrecked ships or stranded whales and porpoises washed up on the sea shore. The tenants also had rights: at Corfe to take underwood from the warren and at Langton Wallis to cut turves from the heath. The tenants had obligations such as to provide carriage for wine, bread and beer from Wareham to the Castle. These were ancient agreements which had existed beyond the memory of man and were jealously guarded by lord and tenant alike. Importantly the customs set the rules of inheritance including the rights of widows to hold their husbands' property and customary tenants to add their children to their tenancies.

As well as the customs associated with Christopher Hatton's manorial lands and tenancies there were customary dues linked to the lordship of Corfe Castle and the Admiralty of Purbeck. These had been set out in the charters that granted the offices and were summarised in English and Latin sections for ease of reference and to show the complete range of his rights.

Customary rights, obligations and payments were standard aspects of Tudor estates. They varied according to local circumstances: not all manors had customs relating to whales and porpoises, but all defined inheritance rights. Sometimes the customs had passed beyond any practical use, but were still recalled as being a right that belonged to the manor: the key to the map of Corfe Castle has a heading "chevage money alias deare month silver" worth 19s. each year. Chevage was a medieval payment made by villeins to leave the manor of their birth – a payment made by the property of the lord to be absent from his workforce – but the tenants in 1586 were personally free so this payment was obsolete. Neither can an occasional payment for absence be an alternative term for 'deare month silver' which is probably a local term for the 'tithing penny' or 'head silver' owed by adult males. The terms have been confused and merged and have lost their original meanings, but remain in an adapted form, for an actual payment.

AREAS OF JURISDICTION

THE WRITTEN SURVEY sets out the areas of jurisdiction over which Sir Christopher Hatton and his tenants had rights or responsibilities. These were multi-layered, they were not usually co-terminous, but neither were they necessarily conflicting if they were clearly defined and lords did not seek to gain access to each other's areas.

In addition to holding a *court baron* the lord sometimes also held a *court leet,* the lowest tier of royal court, attached to some manors and held on the same day as the court baron. The free tenants did not pay homage to the lord of the manor at the court baron, but did recognise the authority of the court leet over which he presided. The court leet could also be attached to a borough court and court leets are still held for Wareham Borough and Portland Manor. Several different lords held manors in Purbeck as well as properties in Corfe Castle borough. Sir Christopher Hatton owned the manors of Langton Wallis and Studland, but other lords held manors in Swanage, Langton Matravers, Worth Matravers and Church Knowle, and each held their own courts.

The manor was the basic area for estate administration, the parish for church administration, and the tithing for legal, military and taxation purposes. The tithing included all of the residents in an area and it was from its members that constables were selected, juries were empanelled to make judgements on minor felonies and weights and measures legislation was enforced at the *court leet.* Tithings such as East and West Tyneham, Povington, East Creech and Church Knowle were outside Hatton's estates; the court leets were held by other lords, but all owed payments towards the provisioning of the Castle, because it defended the whole area. The tithingmen from these tithings, together with those of the tithings within Hatton's manors, were obliged to attend a *hundred court,* which was a royal court with oversight of taxation and military musters.

Hundred courts were administered by the local magnates as franchises: they took a commission from the fines that were imposed and the duties that were charged.

Hatton also held the Purbeck Admiralty through which he was required to maintain national security along the coast and in Poole Bay. The jurisdition of the Admiralty is uncertain as it is not specified in any of the survey or any surviving charters. The importance of the role of Admiral is exemplified in Elizabeth I's charter of 1576. To the east it is unlikely to have extended far into Hampshire and to the west it extended at least as far as Weymouth and probably no further than Lyme Regis. To have responsibility for the defence of a strategic section of the English coast gave Hatton a role which enhanced his position in the Court as it clearly marked him as one of the most trusted of Elizabeth's courtiers.

The survey does not mention any financial benefit that may have been derived from the Admiralty of Purbeck. It had certainly had a considerable value earlier in the century when it was administered by the Crown and the customs duty of 'prisage of wine' yielded over £20 per annum in 1507 and 1508.[5] Although he appointed Francis Hawley as his deputy in Dorset, the post of Admiral ensured that Hatton was drawn into the affairs of the south Dorset coastal towns in court.[6]

LANGTON WALLIS SURVEY OF 1546[7]

A SURVEY COMPILED BY the steward of Langton Wallis in 1546 provides the opportunity for comparison with Treswell's survey a generation later. Like Treswell the steward in 1546 used the local perch of 15 feet and 9 inches as his standard unit of measurement. In 1586 the elderly tenant George Everye held a tenement by a copyhold agreement made 21 March 32 Henry

VIII (1541) which is described in both surveys. Although the copyhold is explicitly the same agreement the descriptions are so different that the details are impossible to reconcile, although the overall acreage of enclosed land is the same:

George Everye's copyhold described in the 1546 survey
One cottage
One close of pasture called Woodclose, 3 acres
One close of pasture called Hethfilde, 5 acres, 2 rods
Three closes of pasture in Norleddes, 15 acres
[Total of enclosed land] 23 acres, 2 rods
Half an acre of meadow
15 acres of arable in the common fields
Common pasture for 15 sheep and 6 [draft] animals

George Everye's copyhold described in the 1586 survey
The house and croft, 2 rods, 10 perches
One close of arable shouting one Langton Common and Brode Downe, 3 acres, 24 perches
One close of pasture shouting one Walter Thomas' Heath field, 7 acres, 1 rod, 16 perches
Two closes of pasture called Morledes, 10 acres, 3 rods, 16 perches
A close adjoining to Bereslade, 1 acre, 3 rods.
Total 23 acres, 2 rods, 26 perches

Treswell's measurements in 1586 are more accurate than those of his predecessor, but he does not include the land pertaining to the copyhold in the common field and meadow or the rights to pasture animals. Neither written survey provides a location for Everye's cottage, but the map shows it in Acton adjacent to the enclosed common fields. Comparison between the two surveys secures a date for the enclosure of the common fields at Langton Wallis between 1546 and 1586. It is rare to be able to date confidently the enclosure of common fields in Dorset to the late sixteenth century, but other examples have been found at Okeford Fitzpaine, Iwerne Courtney, Hinton St Mary and Charminster.[8] That the common fields should have been enclosed at Langton Wallis indicates that the manors in Purbeck were not exempt from the agricultural restructuring which is more usually evidenced in areas were the land was of better quality.

METHOD OF COMPILATION

THE WRITTEN SURVEY contains several features which provide clues as to its method of compilation. Tudor surveys were brought together in several different ways. Richard Wright interviewed the tenants when compiling contemporary surveys for Durweston, Lytchett Minster and Okeford Fitzpaine, giving their names at the start of the surveys to demonstrate that the resulting documents drew upon the traditions of the community.[9] At Sydling St Nicholas an anonymous surveyor consulted the oldest tenants and gave their ages as well as their names.[10]

There is no indication in the text that Treswell consulted the tenants, but the written surveys of lands are dated and clearly contemporary with the cartographic surveys. The charter granted to Hatton in 1576 was summarised in an exemplification dated 1577. This Latin document was included by Treswell as a direct copy from the records in Hatton's muniment room and it seems likely that he drew upon other written records of customary payments and obligations rather than relying entirely on the oral testimony of the tenants and steward.

The final document was written from drafts or assembled manuscripts by a scribe who was not familiar with local personal and place names, as there are several minor errors which would not have been made by a scribe familiar with Purbeck places and families. The surname Cullener, which appears as one of the burgage holders on the map of Corfe Castle, is an error for Culliford, a prominent local family who had been associated with the borough for several generations. Mistakes like this, and the surname Bridges rather than Burges at Middlebere, are those of scribes who were not familiar with the local population.[11] They suggest that Treswell carried out his work as a surveyor alone, or with a team brought from Northamptonshire or London, rather than relying upon local men.

Treswell's survey of Purbeck was undertaken at the same time that he produced a similar manuscript for Hatton's estates in Northamptonshire. He initially worked on the Northamptonshire volume before moving to the Dorset survey, and then returned to revise parts of the Midland survey following estate enclosures, which changed the pattern of the land. It seems most likely that Treswell worked with a team of servants, employees and apprentices collectively amassing documents, consulting local tenants, carrying out surveys and writing drafts under his supervision.

EDITORIAL METHOD, MONEY, WEIGHTS, MEASUREMENTS AND DATES

THE ENGLISH SECTIONS have been transcribed retaining their original word order. Abbreviations have been silently expanded. Archaic forms such as 'holdeth', 'paieth' and 'appeareth' have been transcribed in their more usual modern forms 'holds', 'pays' and 'appears', Substantial Latin sections have been translated and appear in italics, occasional Latin words or phrases have been silently translated and appear in standard font.

Christian names have been standardised with modern spellings. Surnames have been transcribed with their original spellings. Place names have been transcribed with their original spellings.

As far as possible the format of the manuscripts' paragraphs, lists and headings have been retained.

Square brackets have been used to supply additional information such as modern dates, changes in the language of the manuscript, modern place names and obvious scribal errors.

Money: Sums of money and other figures have been standardised as arabic numerals with £ *s. d.* for pounds, shillings and pence.

£1 = 20 shillings
1 *s.* = 1 shilling = 12 pence
1 *d.* = 1 penny
ob. transcribed as ½*d.* = half a penny
1 mark = 13 *s.* 4 *d.*

Denominations that appear in non-standard forms such as 18 *d.* Rather tha 1 *s.* 6 *d.* or 30 *s.* Rather than £1 10 *s.* have been left in their manuscript forms.

Area: Standard areas of land are usually measured in acres, roods and perches
1 acre = 4 roods = 4840 square yards = 0.4 hectares
1 rood = 40 perches = 1210 square yards = 0.1 hectares
1 perch = 5½ square yards = 25.29 square metres

The Purbeck customary acre used by Treswell consisted of 160 square customary perches.[12] Standard perches were 16½ feet in length, but the length of perches varied across the country, and within counties there might be different perches for arable, meadow and woodland. Treswell was careful to note in his written surveys that the perch that he used at Langton Wallis was 15 feet and 9 inches, whereas in Gretton, Northamptonshire, he used a standard perch of 16 feet and 6 inches. The scales on his maps show both the standard perch and the local cutomary perch.

Weight and quantity:

Pound, abbreviated in the text to lb, a unit of weight used for products such as cumin and pepper, in Purbeck the Avoirdupois pound was probably used, equivalent to 454 grams.

Bushel, abbreviated in the text to bsh, a unit of capacity used for grains, equivalent to 8 gallons, probably equivalent to 56 Avoirdupois pounds.

Dates:

The usual form of Tudor dating was the regnal year, adopted as the most common form for dating documents from the thirteenth century, used in private administrations and letters as well as legal documents. This is the form of dating used within the written survey and all of the various charters, leaseholds and copyholds are dated by this method.

Each reign was accepted to have commenced on the day after the previous monarch, so the first day of the reign of Edward VI is 28 January 1547, the day after the death of Henry VIII. Thus the 29 January in the first year of the reign of Edward VI is 29 January 1547, but the 26 January in the first year of the reign of Edward VI is 26 January 1548. Tables to convert regnal years to the modern calendar can be found in Cheney's _Handbook of Dates_.[13]

Mary Tudor's reign introduces a complication following her marriage to Philip of Spain. Her regnal year dates from the death of Edward VI on 6 July 1553, ignoring the nine day reign of Jane, but Philip's reign is added from their marriage on 25 July 1554 so their regnal years are not synchronised. Thus, at Studland, the widow Eleanor Colman held land granted to her deceased husband Nicholas Colman on 26th October in the 5th and 6th years of the reign of Philip and Mary which fell in 1558.

1   Harvey, P. D. A. _Manorial Records,_ British Records Association, revised edition, 1999, pp.15-24. Contempoary guides include: J. Fitzherbert, _The Boke of Surveyeng and Improvementes_ London, 1523, Benese, R. _The boke of measurying of lande as well of woodland as plowland, & pasture in the feelde: & to compt the true nombre of acres of the same,_ Southwark, 1537 and reprinted at least three times during the sixteenth century.

2   Palmer, J. _Three Tudor Surveys: The Dorset manors of Sir Thomas Kitson: Okeford Fitzpaine, Durweston cum Knighton and Lytchett Minster,_ Dorchester, Dorset Record Society, vol. 18, 2015.

3   Nottingham University Library, manuscripts department, reference: Mi/M/223.

4   Forrest M. _Dorset Manorial Docuements: a guide for local and family historians,_ Dorchester, Dorset Record Society, Occasional Papers 2, 2011. Bettey J. H. 'Marriages of Convenience by Copyholders in Dorset during the 17th Century', _Proceedings of the Dorset Natural History and Archaeological Society,_ 1976, vol.98, pp.1-5.

5   The National Archives, references: SC6/HenVII/1234 and 1235.

6   Brooks E. St. J. _Sir Christopher Hatton: Queen Elizabeth's Favourite,_ London, 1946, pp.116-7.

7   Nottingham University Library, manuscripts department, reference: Mi/M/223.

8   Palmer, _Three Tudor Surveys,_ particularly pp.32-35. C. Taylor _The Making of the English Landscape: Dorset,_ second edition, Wimborne, 2004, pp.127-130.

9   Palmer, _Three Tudor Surveys,_ pp. 67, 118 and 144.

10 Forrest M. 'A Broad Sydling Survey' _Somerset and Dorset Notes and Queries,_ 2013,vol.37, pp.221-4.

11 The Bridges (rather than Burges) family appear in a lease of 1620 which extended their tenure to the property at Middlebere granted in 1573, Dorset History Centre, reference: D/BKL/A/F/33.

12 Dilley R. S. 'The Customary Acre: an indeterminate measure' _Agricultural History Review,_ 1975, vol.23, pp.173-6.

13 Cheney, C. R. ed. _Handbook of Dates for Students of English History,_ Cambridge, 1945.

FACSIMILE

The Treswell Survey, Dorset History Centre reference D/BKL/E/A/3/1, consists of Ralph Treswell's maps and survey, John Hawsted's map and Christopher Saxton's map with later annotations.

All folios containing text have been reproduced on the following pages, including the cover and front end board. The folios each measure 16½ inches x 10¾ inches.

The first three folios have no contemporary numbering. Thereafter each folio is numbered consecutively 1-50 in the top right corner followed by three blank folios.

The following folios are blank and have not been reproduced in this volume:
1 verso (v.) – 2 recto (r.), 3v. - 4r., 10v. - 11r., 17v. - 18r., 24v. - 25r., 41v. - 42r., 44v. - 45r., 49v.- end.

Maps of Dorsetshire —
Purbeck, Corfe Castle & Grounds adjoining —
Ground Plan of Corfe Castle — Drawing of the Upright
of Corfe Castle — and a Map of the Town of Corfe Castle
and adjoining Grounds. by Treswell and Treswell —
Surveys of the four Manors in Purbeck
of Corfe Castle, Mudland Langton Worth and
Eastington; &c taken in 1585, 1586, and 1724.

April the 26th 1697 Memorandum That this Book was
Established and produced on the Examinacõn of a Comission
out of the Court of Yorkshire for Examining Witnesses
in a Cause there depending between Anthony Ettrick Esq
Complt and John Pyke Gent. Defendt touching the Examinacõn
of Henry Robbins a Witness for the Complt and that
relacõn to him

Tho: Byres

Williams

Geo: Duke

Our Sovereign Lord the King in his Office of
Admiralty against Forty nine Casks of Brandy found
derelict on the High Seas and brought to or near
Poole And also against William John Bankes Esquire
the Sole Executor of the Will of Henry Bankes Esquire
deceased intervening and claiming to be entitled
to forty three of the said Casks of Brandy.

———————

This is the Book referred to or described as Document
No 2 in the joint Affidavit of William Castleman and
Henry Castleman made in the above Cause and sworn
the second day of November 1835. Before me

Edward Castleman
a Master Extra in Chancery

TANDEM · SI ·

Contents

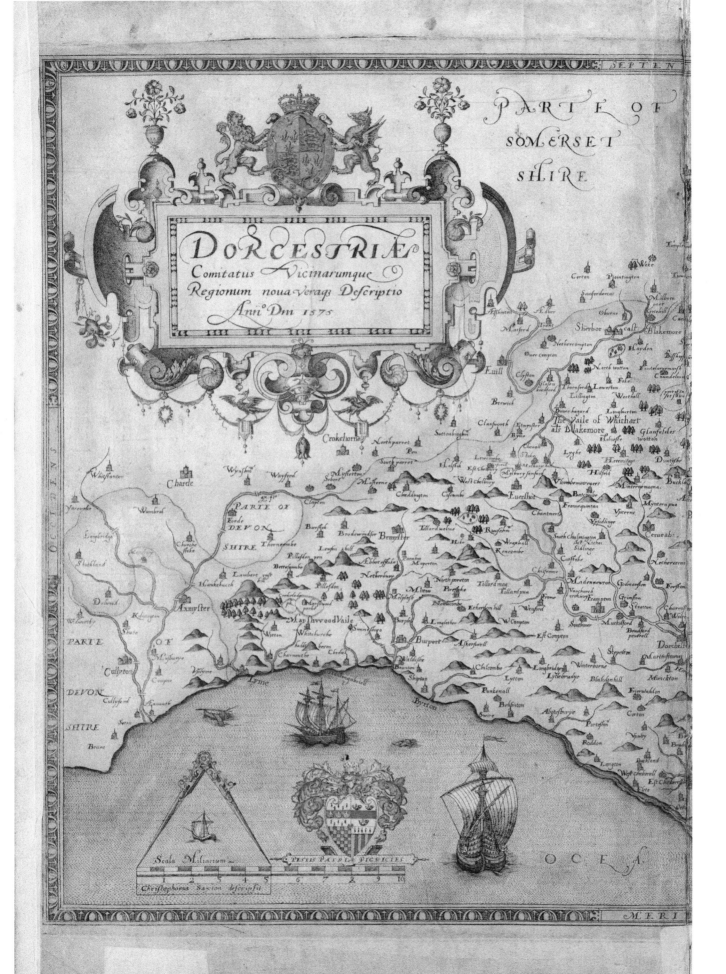

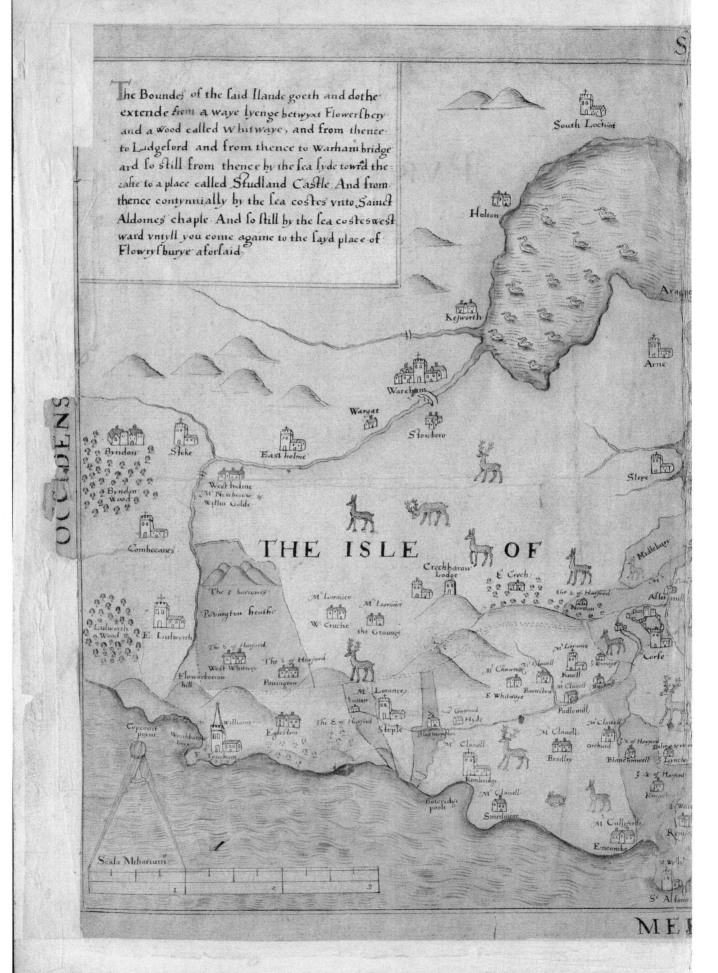

The Boundes of the said Ilande goeth and dothe
extende from a waye lyenge betwyxt Flowersbery
and a wood called Whitwaye, and from thence
to Ludgeford and from thence to Warham bridge
and so still from thence by the sea syde towrd the
easte to a place called Studland Castle And from
thence contynnially by the sea costes vnto Sainct
Aldomes chaple And so still by the sea costes west
ward vntyll you come againe to the sayd place of
Flowrysburye aforsaid.

South Lochiot

Holton

Aragge

Kesworth

Arne

Wareham

Wargat

Stowboro

Slepe

Byndon

Stoke

East holme

West holme
Mr Newberew &
Willm Golde

Combecanes

Midlebury

THE ISLE OF

Crechbarow
Lodge

E Crech

Aflet mill

Lulworth
Wood

E Lulworth

The 5 barrowes

Povington heathe

Mr Lorance

Mr Lorance

W Cruche

the Graunge

Nordon

The E of Harford

Mr Lorance

Mr Chawtell

Mr Clauell

Knoll

Donage

Corfe

The E of Harford

West Whitwey

The E of Harford

Povington

Mr Clauell

Barnston

E Whitwaye

Mr Clauell

Buckhell

Sutton

Mr Lorance

Steple

Padlemill

Mr Clauell

Copcourt
poynt

Wemhharow
baye

williams

Egleston

The E of Harford

Blashmorton

Hyde

Mr Clauell

Mr Clauell

Orchard

The E of Harford

Blanchmwell

S Lynche

E Lyncham

Kimbridge

Bradley

The E of Harford

Kengst

Boterdge
poole

Mr Clauell

Smedmore

Mr Cullyford

Kengs

Encombe

St Aldams

Scala Miliarium

1   2   3

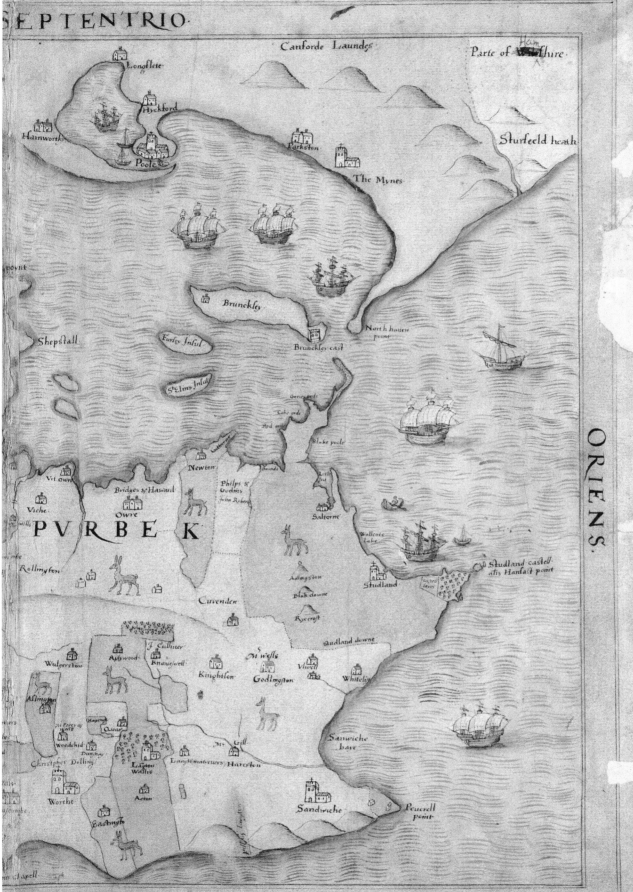

83

Canforde Laundes

Parte of Wiltshire.

Longflete

Hyckford

Hainworth

Poole

Parkston

The Mynes

Sturfeeld heath

Brunckley

Furfey Infula

Shepstall

Brunckley cast

North hauen poine

St Elms Infula

Geric yate

Coho yate

Red milk

Blake poole

Newton

Lutlesoune

Little fea

Vit. owrt

Bridges & Hainnul

Philps & Godms

John Rohers

Viche

Owre

Saltorne

PVRBEK

Wallcote lake

Studland castell, alis Hanfast point

Rollington

Admyston

Studland

Ludland leven

Black downe

Cuvenden

Rycroft

Studland downe

J. Culliuer

Aftwood

St wests

Wulgerston

Knaue well

Knightson

Godlmyston

Viuell

Whitelin

Aftmston

St Percy & Godl

Hanly

Quar

Weedchid

Dunshay

Christpher Dollng

Mr. Grill

Sanwiche bare

Layton Wallis

Langtomatreuers

Haresteu

Worthe

Acton

Sandwiche

Peuerell point

Eastnyst

ORIENS.

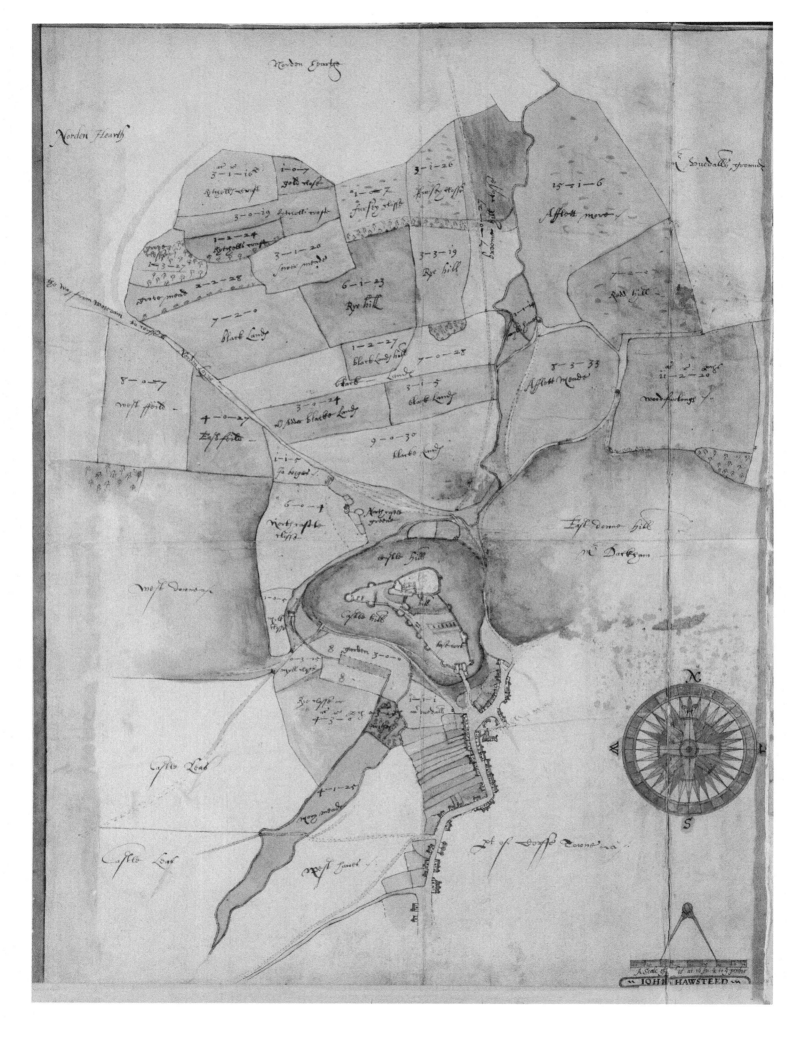

CORFE CASTLE;

The Seconde Warde

The Thirde
Warde

The Dungen
Towre

Newe
Bulwark

The Kinges

a valuce

The leave leading
vp vnto ye brige Towre

the bridge

OCCIDENS

A Scale of

Radius Prefens

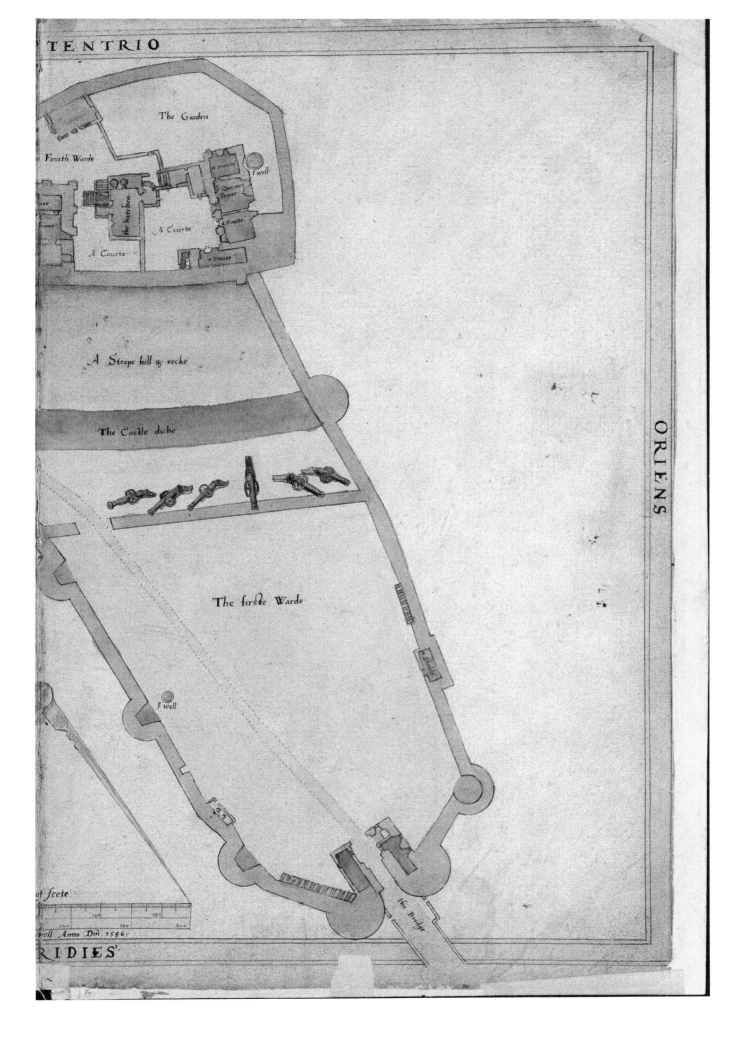

SEPTENTRIO

The Garden

The Fourth Warde

a wall

Queene's Tower

The kitchen

A Courte

A Courte

a Vaute

a Vaute

§ well

§ well

A Steepe hill & rocke

The Castle diche

The firste Warde

§ well

ORIENS

The Bridge

of feete

140   160   180   200

...rell Anno Dni 1586

...RIDIES

CORFE,

the river from

NORDON

Nordon

Nordon Wood

Nordon downe

The hill

Knoll downe

Bucknoll downe

B

Parsonadge downe

Castle do

Lounge close

pasture

hill close

pasture

The Parsonage ground

V

pasture

Bucknoll grove

pasture & Wood

Wood

pasture

knoll

pasture

Dattomb
a close

KNOLL

knoll

Meadow

C

pasture

the Prebend

knoll

pasture

Z

pasture

South close

Kingst

O

pasture

L

pasture

pasture

pasture

Bucknoll
farme

pasture

L

pasture

Meadow

pasture

The

meadow

ORCHARDE

kingston

Norleys common to kingston

kingston

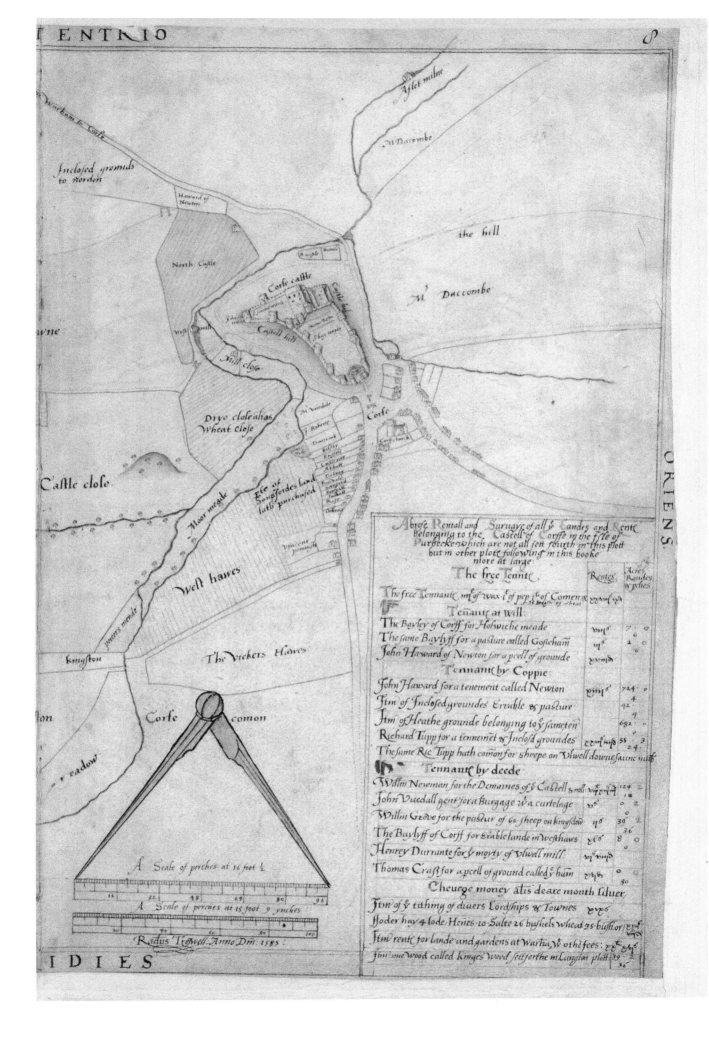

NEWTON;

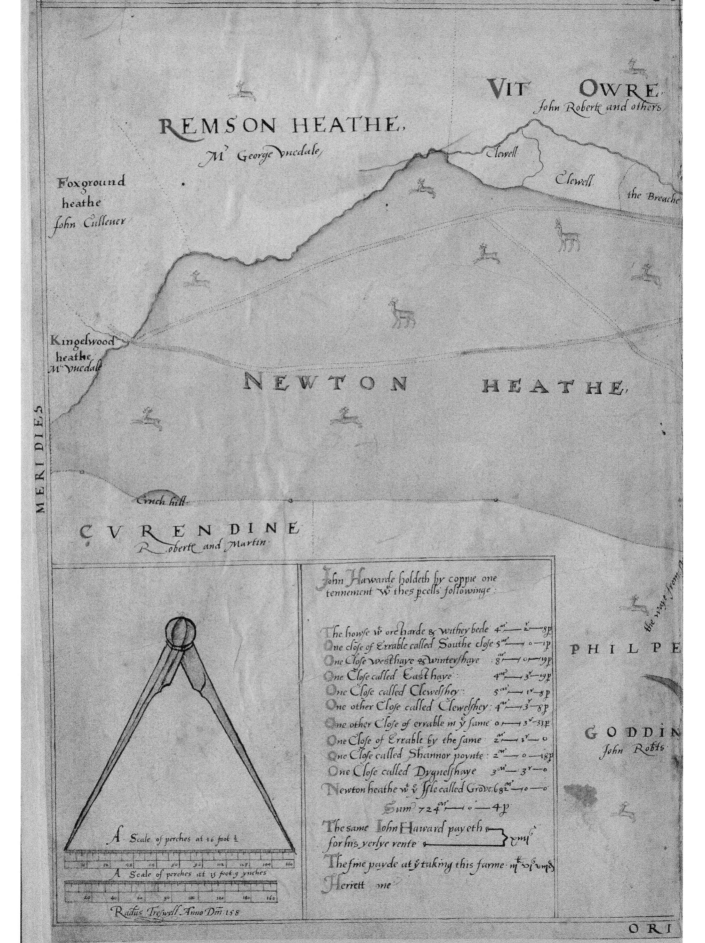

REMSON HEATHE,

M.ʳ George Vnedale,

VIT OWRE,
John Roberte and others

Foxground
heathe
John Culleuer

Clewell

Clewell.

the Breache

Kingelwood
heathe
M.ʳ Vnedale

NEWTON HEATHE,

MERIDIES

Crich hill

CVRENDINE
Roberte and Martin

PHILPE

GODDIN
John Robts

the waye from

John Haward holdeth by coppie one
tennement wᵗ thes pcells followinge:

The howse wᵗ orcharde & withey bede	4ᵃᶜ	2	8p
One close of Errable called Southe close	5ᵃᶜ	0	1p
One Close westhaye & wintershaye	8ᵃᶜ	0	19p
One Close called Easthaye	4ᵃᶜ	3	19p
One Close called Clewelshey	5ᵃᶜ	1	8p
One other Close called Clewelshey	4ᵃᶜ	3	8p
One other Close of errable in ẙ same	0	3	33p
One Close of Errable by the same	2ᵃᶜ	1	0
One Close called Shannor poynte	2ᵃᶜ	0	18p
One Close called Drynelshaye	3ᵃᶜ	3	0
Newton heathe wᵗ ẙ Isle called Grove	682ᵃᶜ	10	0

Sum 724ᵃᶜ 10 4p

The same John Haward payeth
for his yerlye rente ︙ vm

The sme payde at ẙ taking this farme inᵗ xvimᵈ

Herriett one

A Scale of perches at 16 foot ½

A Scale of perches at 15 foot 9 ynches

Radius Treswell Anno Dm 158

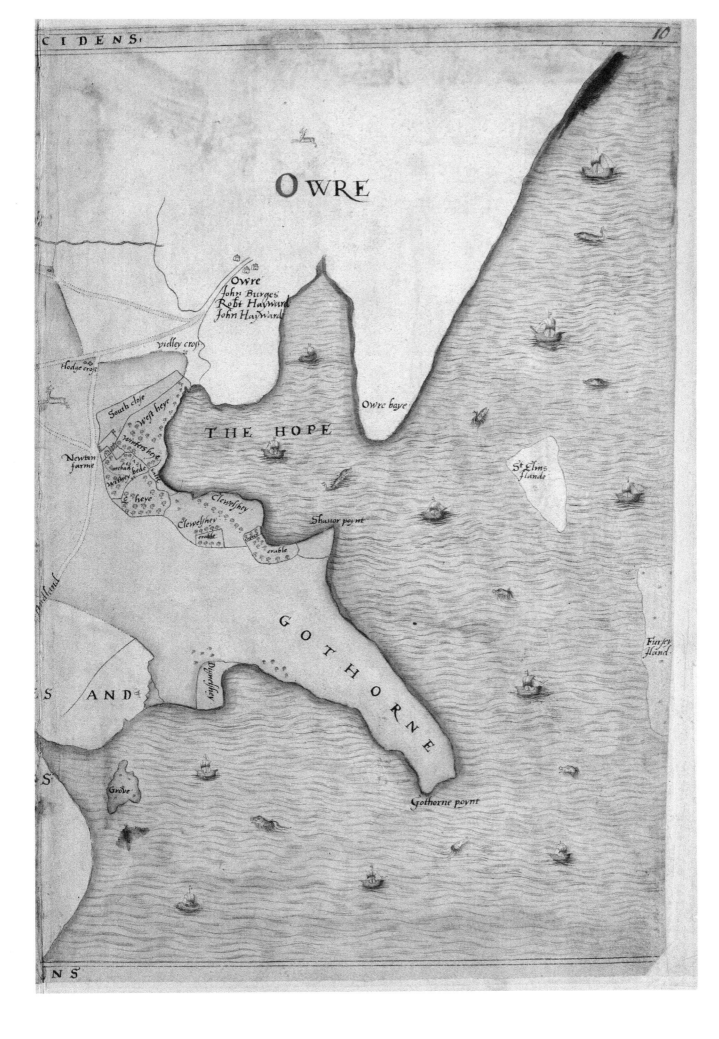

OWRE

Owre
John Burges
Robt Hayward
John Hayward

Vidley cross

Hodge cross

South close

West heye

Winters heye

Newton farme

orchard

Withey hede

heye

Clewelshey

Clewelshey

erable

erable

THE HOPE

Owre baye

Shauor poynt

St Elms flande

Fursey flande

GOTHORNE

Dymelshey

AND

Grove

S

Gothorne poynt

NS.

Memorand. that at a Court holden at Wareham in the county of Dorsett on Thursday the one and twentieth day of Aprill 1698 for the examinacon of witnesses in a Cause depending in his Ma:ties high Court of Chauncery betweene George Pitt Esq: compl.t and John Bankes Esq: one of the Deft:s to the bill of Compl.t of the said George pitt This written paper booke was shewed forth unto Rob.t Russell gent and Peter Mayor produced and sworne on the part and behalf of the said Deft: John Bankes before us.

Roder

John Ruthcliff

Ne: Ingram

Mem.d That at a Comission held att Corffe Castle in the Isle of Purbecke County of Dorsett on Munday the twentieth day of December in the one & twentieth yeare of the Raigne of King Charles the Second for the examinacon of witnesses in a Cause depending in his Mat: high Court of Chauncery betweene S.r Ralph Banks Kn.t Complaynt and Thom.s Dollinge Widdow & others Defendts this written paper Booke was shewed forth unto John Randall gent produced & sworne on the part and behalfe of the Complaynt before us

Robert: Culliforde.

Tho: Baynard

Edm: Aubrey.

12

The Survaye of the mannor of Corfe

with the castle called Corfe castle in the Isle
of Purbecke, in the countye of Dorsett, with
the honoers Landes, Rightes, Customes, and
Sordres belonging to the same, made in Anno
Dm .1586.

Free holders

The manor of Corfe holdeth the pesage of woll & Cheese
throwgh the whole Isle for the which het paieth yearly to the
lorde of the Castell two ponde of waxe price viij at ye feaste of
St. michell Arch.

ij^lb of waxe price
vij d.

William Darombe gent holdeth on close of pasture
late the landes of the psone of Corfe conteyning i^er called tolers crose
& payeth yearly one pond of waxe price iij at ye feast aforesaid

i^lb of waxe price
vij d.

Robarte Sollinge in free sorrage one Burgage late
Rich. Phillips & payeth yearlie therfore at ye feaste aforesaid

vij d.

Henry Unedall Esquier holdeth freely in Sorrage
Certaine landes and Tenements in Corffe Castell
and payeth yearly at the feaste afore said.

vij d.

The Same Henry houldeth certaine landes &
Tenements in Kadlingtoy als Kotlingtony to him & his
heyres and payeth yearlye Twentie horse showes
for Frome at ye feaste afort said

xx horshowes of
yon price
xxd.

The same Henry and John Sanforde holdeth certaine
water course leadinge to the mill called brode mill and paith
therfore yearely Twentie Sesternes of Ale euerye
Sesterne contayning Twentie Gallons price vj viij^d
at the election of the Constable at ý feaste aforesayde.

{ xx Sesternes of
Ale price
vjs viij^d

John Trewe holdeth freely certaine landes & tenementh
called north Castell with in the boroughe of worst
and paith therfore yearly at the feaste aforesaid

{ iiij^d

The same John holdeth a nother close in the weste
parted of the close of henry Bonvile there late kinhad
knight & paieth yearlie at the feast aforesayde

{ dim of dimyn price
iiij^d

Henry Bonvill holdeth freely one close of pasture
conт. x lynge besides the bridge called Edwardes bridge
And paieth yearely at the feast Aforesayd

{ dim of dimyn price
iiij^d

John Hayword holdeth freely on Burgage late
Steuey Haywarde & paith yearly therfore at the feast
aforesaide two horsshewes of Iron with nailed price

{ ij horsshowes of
Iron price
iiij^d

John Cobanh in the right of mary his wife holdeth
freely one Burgage in worst late Thomas higell
father of the saide marie & paieth yearly vj^d and also
he holdeth certaine Landes and Tenementh called
Clewell & paith yearly at the feaste aforesaide ij^s vj^d

{ iiij^d

13

William Dacombe gent holdeth freelie one Close of meadow
called Piper Crosse Contayning three acres and paieth
yearely at the feast aforesaid ——————————————— ijs

John Sanford holdeth freelie one Close of pasture called
Longe Evall and payeth yearlie at the feast aforesaid ——— vjd

John Tye holdeth freelie one Burgage and one Close called
Digtarys haye and payeth yearely at ye feaste aforesaid ——— viijd

Henrye Bowdich holdeth freelie one Shoppe late
Cooked and payeth therefore yearly at the feast aforesaid ——— ijd

The same Henry holdeth freelie three Burgages
in Dorse and payeth yearely at ye feaste aforesaid ——————— viijd

Thomas Rye holdeth freely one Burgage in west
Streete & paieth yearly at the feast aforesaid ————————————— ijd

Robarte Devonmiter holdeth freely one Shoppe late
Thomas Hoopers & payeth therefore yearly at ye feast aforsaid ——— ijd

Henrye Welleb in the right of marie his wife daughter
and heare of John pole holdeth freely one burgage with the
apptur late Normans & paieth yearlie at the feast aforesaid ——— iijd

John Barron holdeth frelie certaine landes & Burgages and payeth yearlie iij^d and j^lb off waxe price vj^d at the feast afore &c. — ij^d j^lb off waxe price vj^d iiij^d

Wm William Trewe holdeth frely a certaine prcell off lande called Corse mans grounde lat Kirk whittles & paieth yearlie — ij^d

The tenementes off Nordey in the pishe off Corse paieth yerly at Michellmas by Auntient Custome Twentie horse shewes off Iron with nailes now praysed at — xx horsesheues off Iron price xx^d

The tennauntes off the mann̄o off Over in ye pish off Corse payeth yearelie for iij horssheues off Iron w^t nailes off Auntiente Custome as appereth in the Custom̄ary — iij horsheues off Iron w^t nailes price vj^d

Sum xxxvj^s iiij^d { j^lb off waxe j^lb off Common j^lb off peper } iij^lb xij^s

14

2. Teunantes at will

The Bailiffe of the Burrouge of Corfe for the tyme beinge by vertue of his office holdeth one meadow called holwich meade Contayninge vij Acres and payeth yearly at the feaste of St michell the Arkangell /

vij[s]

The same Bayliffe for the time beinge holdeth the pasture of one Close called gosse hame Contayning twaacres and payeth yearly therefore /

iiij[s]

John Hayward of newton holdeth at will a certaine prell of Landes and paieth therefore yearly Two Busshells of Salte price vij[d] & three hennes price vj[d]

xvij[d]

Sum xv[s] vij[d]

3. Tennentes By coppie of courte role /

John Hayward holdeth one tenemente with Cottage and diuers closes & prells of lande hereafter followeth w[th] happurtenannce in newton in the p[ar]ishe of Studelande together w[th] A licence to take berdes or fowle as well in the Lordes Comon and vpon the Coosted or vyner of the Sea there and paieth therefore yearly /

xiiij[s] & j [illegible]

John Haywarde

The House with the Orcharde and one Parcell off grounde called withit heade	4li — 2s — 8d
One close off pasture called weste heye and Winters haye	8li — 0 — 19d
One other close off pasture called Easte haye	4li — 3s — 19d
One other close off pasture adioyning to the same called Clewellheye	5li — 1s — 8d
One other close one the weste syde the same called Clewellheye	4li — 3s — 8d
Ane other close off Erable in the same	2li — 3s — 3d
One Close off Earable adioyninge vpon Clewellhey	2li — 1s — 0
One other close lyinge nexte the same called Shannorpoynte	2li — 0 — 18d
One close called dignellhaye	3li — 3s — 0
The heathe called newton heathe with the prell off ground called grone	682li — 0 — 0
One Close off Erable called South close	5li — 0 — 1d
	724li — 0 — 1d

Richarde Tuppe holdeth one tenemente with divers

Closes and prell off lande in solwell downe and in the parrishe off Sanwich with commoy off pasture vpon solwell Downe and wichtly downe for sheepe without number with the Appurtenances late in the tenor off Thomas Leyde & paieth therefore yearly

xvij li d
C. forbett

One tenemente with A curtellage garden orchard & croste	3li — 3s — 25d
One close called Ridge acre	3li — 1s — 24d ob
One close called Hille combe	2li — 2s — 29d
One close called Tille haye	0 — 2s — 20d
One close called whitleyes	1li — 0 — 0
One close called Tonthills by tonthills land	1li — 0 — 20d
ffower closes called new close and a litle close	19li — 0 — 36d
One close called brome Hill	3li — 3s — 21d

15

One close off meadowe called brooke meadowe ———————— | i^s — iv — 12½
One close off meadowe called mill hayes ———————— | o — 3s — 15½

with common off pasture on Shwell downe & whitley downe
for beasted without number

Sum xxxvij iij d | 35^ii — 3s — 24½ ½

1. **Tennantes by deede**

William Nerman off poole by ye assignacion
off John Moyle Esquier holdeth by lettre patents
for tearme off certaine yeares yett induringe all ye
demaines landes off ye Castell or lordshipe off Dorse
aforesaide and also one Griste mill in Dorse aforesaid
and also all houses buildinges dove houses Orchardes
gardeines watters water courses fishinges and
all other profitts commodities and emollumente
to ye saide mill belonging with the appurten and
paieth yearlie therefore | xvij^ii iij d

One Close off meadowe called moore meadow | 5^on — o —10½
One other pcell off meadowe called porters meadow | 1^on — o — o
One close off pasture called white close | 7^on — o — o
One close off arable called mill close | 2^on — o — o
One close off pasture called castle close or castle leyes | 59^on — o — o
One close off pasture called castle downe | 46^on — o — o
One close off pasture called castle Burowgh | 4^on — 2^s — o
And all that mill aforesaid | Sum 124^on—2s—10½

John Rudall gent holdeth for terme off yeares
yett induring one Burgage in the towne off Dorse
wth A Curtelage adioyning cont by estimacion
halfe an acer wth the app^tu late in the tenure off
Thomas Browne and payeth yearly therfore | ij^s

4

William Croue holdeth the pasture off three scoure sheepe
uppon kings woode downe vnto the lordes woode called kings woode
Annexed p̃cell off the lordes deymagned and paieth therefore yearly ⎬ 36ᵗⁱ — 2 — 36p.
vjᵈ

The Baylisse off Corfe yeldeth for eaighte Acres off arable
grounde lyeng in the comm̃ey feilde off Corfe called the weste
hawed late purchased off John Samforde & paieth yearly ⎬ 8ᵘˢ — 0 — 0
xlᵈ

Henery Durrante holdeth the moietie off one grise mill
at Ohwell and payeth therefore yearly ⎬ vjˢ viijᵈ

Thomas Crasse holdeth to him Anne his wife and william
there sonne for terme off there lives A Certaine p̃cell off lande
called the Cany contayning by Estimation 30 p̃ches & payeth yearly — ⎬ 0 — 0 — 30 p.
xijᵈ

The Wood called kinges woode set forth in Langton walles
plott contayntg: / 39ᵗⁱ — 2ˢ — 36 p.

　　　　　Sum xⁱⁱ vjˢ iiijᵈ

　　　　Mounye Due and payable to the Castell off /
　　　Corfe yearly by the inhabitantes off the Isle /
　　　off purbecke to be collected by the gouernour /
　　　off the Londe Isle with certaine
　　　　　Haye Henes Salte
　　　　　and Corne as /
　　　　　followeth /

The tythinge off herston ＿＿＿＿＿＿＿＿＿＿ vjᵈ
The tythinge off whitclosse ＿＿＿＿＿＿＿＿ vjᵈ
The tythinge off Langton wallis ＿＿＿＿＿＿ vjᵈ

16

The tythinge off worth ⸺⸺⸺⸺⸺⸺⸺ vj d
The tythinge off Assington ⸺⸺⸺⸺⸺⸺ vj d
The tythinge off Pollington ⸺⸺⸺⸺⸺⸺ vj d
The tythinge off Burstow ⸺⸺⸺⸺⸺⸺ vj d
The tythinge off Axemcombe ⸺⸺⸺⸺⸺ vj d
The tythinge off Bradhe farme ⸺⸺⸺⸺⸺ vj d
The tythinge off One tenemente in weste Orcharde off the
Inheritaunce off John Clauell Esquier now in the occupation } iiij d
off John Gould
The tythinge off on tenementes off william Chaltottes gent in } iiij d
west Orcharde
The tythinge off one tenements in weste Orcharde aforesaide } iiij d
latly purchased by John Clauell Esquier off Symond davye
The Tythinge off knowle ⸺⸺⸺⸺⸺⸺⸺⸺ vj d
The tythinge off Easte critch ⸺⸺⸺⸺⸺⸺ vj d
The tythinge off Eagalstone ⸺⸺⸺⸺⸺⸺ vj d
The tythinge off Easte Tynehame ⸺⸺⸺⸺ vj d
The tythinge off weste Tynehame ⸺⸺⸺⸺ vj d
The tythinge off povington ⸺⸺⸺⸺⸺⸺ vj d
Goldstone pcell off the tythinge off afflingtone ⸺⸺⸺ vj d

Sum vij s

Fodee Haye

Godlingstone for one lode off Haye called fodder Haye ⸺⸺ vj d

The tithing off herstony a lode off Haye or ij s ⸺⸺⸺ vj d

Williame knige many for his laundes in newtony A } vj d
lode off Haye or ij s ⸺⸺⸺⸺⸺⸺⸺⸺

The tenamente off the landes called woodeheade a lode off haye ij s   vj d

Sum vm s

Hennes

Godlingston for the price of ij hennes ———————— iiijd

Phitworth for the price of vj hennes ———————— vjd

Philpes in the fearme for the price of ij henns ———— iiijd

Sum xxd

Salte

Godlingston for the price of two bushells of salte ——— vijd

Phitworth for the price of vj bushells of salte ——— ijs

Philpes in the fearme for the price of ij bushells of salte —— vijd

Meddlebery for the price of ij quarters of salte ———— viijs

Sum vijs

Wheate

The farme of Langton walld of wheate ————————— vj Buz.

The farme of Sutton of wheat ————————— xvj Buz.

The farme of worth of wheate ————————— viij Buz.

Sum xxx Buz.

17

Monnye paide to the Castell towarde the Rangers and Keepers wages

Donington ——————————————— xxvs

Worth ——————————————— xxxs

Langton Wallis ——————————————— xxvjs

Godlingstone for monny called Suttons fyne ——— ijs

Sum' iiijli Sum

Wareham without the Isle of Purbecke

18w — 0 — 0	Frannces Hawlie esquier for the meadowes ther by the yeare ——— viijd
1ar — 2v — 0j	Xpofer Anketell esquier for a close called castell close yearly at midd ——— vs
	John Townde for one garden at michelmas ——————— vjd
	Frannces Stevard for one garden at millane as before ——— vjd viijd
	William Lane one garden by the personage house of St martaine iiijd yerly ——— vijd
	John Jervey one garden at millane yearly ——————— vvijd
	John Rodgers one garden at michells lane yearly ——————— vvijd
	George Stevarde for one garden by Alhallon well yearly ——— vijd
	Nicolas Stevarde for one garden at Butsherde ——————— vvijd
	The same nicolas for an other garden called crooked garden alholowell ——— ijs
	The same for an other garden by harvies howse in westreete adioyning to the personage of St michell ——— iiijd
	The fisshing of the north river and south river there Nicholas Eliz ——— xxvijs
	The fee of the Baylywicke of wayemonth wyke Hellwell portland and wareham togeder with the hundreds of Lambrowge rinnove and Hasellor yp Anno ——— vjli

Sum xvjli xvjs

The abridgemente

of certein Libtyes ptayninge to
the Castle off Corffe in the Ile off Purberke, in the Countye
off Dorsett, conteyned in the Olde Charter off the saide
Castell, with the boundes of the Ilande

The Bondres,

off the same Ilande goeth and doth extende from a way
lyinge betwixt fflowresberye and a wade called Whitwaye, and from thence
to Ludy forde, and from thence to warehame bridge, and so still from thence
by the sea syde toward the East to a place called Studland Castle, And
so from thence continnallye by the sea coste unto St Aldons raple
and so still by the sea coste westward, untill you come to the said place off
fflowresberye aforesaide.

Item that the whole Ilande is a warren, and apperteyneth to the Castle

Item, that all pleces off, Deart Denyson and wreake off the sea appteyneth to the Castle
and determinable by the Constable and his Steward, and the fynes thereof
pteyneth to the Constable

Item that all Straungers as well off the warren as elsewhere, being attach, within
the boundes off the Ilande for any trespas done shall have Justice and
answere before the Constable and in no other Courte

Item yff any off the towne off Corffe do complayne to the Const or Maior off Corffe
uppon any dwellinge within the warren aforesaide, either for debte or
other offence, the same ought to be attached by warren sworne, and come
and answere at the next hundred Courte off Corffe, before the Constable
and in no other Courte and the Constable shall have the amryamient

Item that the Lorde off the Castle shall have thne moytye off all ransod ptayninge
to the Bishopp or Archbishopp within the whole pishe off Corffe, And the
Bishopps or Archbishopps officers cominge thither to have ransck or matie
shall see their greyhoundes run at the hare by the deue off the Warener

Item, yff there be Cartes within the towne off Corffe, able to carry a whole
tunne off wine, the owners off the Cartes shall carry for the Constable
yearly, from wareham to the Castle, two tunne off wine, and the
Carryers shall have for every tunne cariage, 4d, and his Corrody
honorable.

Item that the men of Corffe ought to receave prisoners sent to the Castle by the Kinges Commaundement at Wareham bridge, and so with the Constables ayde carrye them to the Castle, and when they shalbe sent agayne to any other prison, they shall bringe them agayne to the same bridge with the like ayde

Item yf any warre happen nigh the Castle, the tenauntes of the Towne aforesaid by the tenure of their Lande ought to be in the Castle by the space of xl tj dayes at their owne propre costes for the defence of the same Castle

Item that the Tenauntes of the Towne of Corffe and carte every Saterday to carry for the Constable bread and beare from Wareham to Corffe and the Drivers of the Cart shall have their Corrady of the Constable or else iij d

Item that the Constable shall take the assise of Ale, that ys to say, vij gallons of Ale for iij d a bushell within the towne, as without through the whole warren, so that there halfe be of the best and the other of the second sort

Item that no inholder bringe flysshe within the warren shall carry the same fishe out of the saide warren, but that he pitche the same first at the crosse of Corffe tarrynge there to sell the same by the space of an hower, and making default and taken flyinge shall lose his fysshe at the Constables pleasure

Item at the reames of every Constable the warrenner shall somon iiij men of every of the tithinges of Brinkesley and Dwrit to come to Corffe, before the Constable there in full court, to be sworne nether to conveye out, nor bringe into the warren any hunters or other evill doers

Item that no owners of any woodes within the warren maye cutt or carry awaye any of their woodes, without the oversight of the warren but in this order yf they aske leave of the warryner and cannot obtayne leave then they must come to the Castle gate with witnes of some of the townes men declaring the same to the porter and aske leave, And that done and approved they shalbe discharged yf they happen to be attached

Item that the Constable tyme out of mans remembraunce hath had the prysage of wine of every shippe arrivinge upon the sea coast of Purbecke yf the shipp there do tarry and doe stay for selle with Cordes and Ankers in the right of the Lord of the Castle

Item that the Constable tyme out off mynde hath had the wreakes off the
sea throughe his whole bayly wyrke when they happened

Item that the Lorde hath had tyme out off mynde all Regall or hedfisshes as
Grasped Porpeyes and Sturgeon taken upon the sea roste off Purbeck

Item that the Lord hath had all ffalcons Eyenge or breedinge upon the Baylywyrke
aforesaide but the Constable is wont to reward the takers off the said
ffisshes and ffalcons

Liberties off the Towne off Corffe

Item that the whole Towne off Corffe apperteyneth to the Castle, and the tennts
off the same Towne are called Barons, and are as free as the Barons
off the fyve portes. But they can holde no plees but off J deponders
but all their presentments and termynacons are before the Constable
and his stuarde with the amerciments rominge off the same

Item that the Court off Corffe ought not to be kept but from 3 weekes to
3 weekes, except the Queenes writt happen to come

Item to the Towne off Corffe belonge all judiciall as iyms poles and belly and
all pleas th apperteyne to the kinge and dignitye off his Crowne
So that the same be determyned here before the kinge Justices

Item that by the comme assent thinhercios off Corffe doo yearely chuse amonge
them selues at the Lawdaye holden for the Towne, at the feast off
Saint Michaell tharcanngell A Maior, Two Coromdon Beadle
and two Tasters

The Customes off the Towne off Corffe

Item The Maior off Corffe hath used to hunt by Custome the Deare or any
other game yearly upon Maye daye, accompayned with his brethren
the Maisters off the Towne; Inheritours off the flande and other yout
off the Comitye th shall happen to come, in all places off the
Countesyde off the Castle and greate Dorone

Item that the Maior off Corffe hath hade by the Custome yearly, and the
whole yeare one horse to goe and depasture in the Castle grownd
for the service off the prime as it is his plege

Item that the free barons and inheritours off Corffe ought to digge and haue
turves throughe the whole warren, without the denyall of any
person And that they ought to drine their Cattagle to holme
mounte in the west walke, on whitsondaye yearely them to depasture
that daye and three dayes followinge

Certaine Customes and Orders belonginge to the Castle to

be approved by the Court Rolles and Comon Use /

Itm̄ there apperteyneth to the Castle of Corffe 2 Lawdayes yearly to be kept
at the Castle gate called the owte Lawdayes, beinge of the nature of
a ned courte, or Swaynimote Courte, the one kept at the feast
of St Michaell tharchangle, the other at the feast of thannunc͂on
of our Ladye, whereunto doth appeare all the free holders of
the Ilande, and all the Tethinge men of all the 2 Hundredds of
Rouge barrow and Hasillor, with there posts and Tythmen, some
with 5 fiue, fower, three or two, as appeareth by records /

Itm̄ There are Two small Lawdayes for the Towne, kept at the termes
and place aforesaide by the Constable officer /

Itm̄ The Constable officer and Steward may keepe every iij weeke a
Courte called Hundred Courte, wherein are tryed, writts of Ryght
pleas of Tresspas and debt, and all other comon pleas and at their
courte be made presentm͂t of thoffenders against the game, and
of Deart and Vreakes by the Rauyer and Warinders of Purbecke
aswell in the Lawedayes wherin the Warin̄ is the officer to execute
proces, and to present all measure weyght and bread, and other officers /

Itm̄ Euery fisscherman within the Ilande, at euery Lawdaye payeth to the
Castle for lieue to fisshe for euery boate iiijd, And the tethingman
presenteth the boate of euery tethinge and all manner wreakes, and
Dedaundes happeninge within their seuerall tethinge to /

These customes need
no proffe for that
they are in dayly
use /

Other Customes and orders aproued by the
Court Rolles /

Itm̄ that no Ilander ought to marye his Doughter out of the Ilande, without
lieue of the Lord Constable or other officer /

Itm̄ that no Inhabiton of the Ilande shall make any Stonewall Hedge or
Dytche alone the assise that is no Higher, then that a Hind with
her Calfe may easely leape ouer at all places /

Itm̄ that no man ought to take or hunt any Conyes, Hare, ffox, or ffesaunte
with Dogges nettes or ferryalls within the warren, without lieue
or vewe of the warein /

Itm̄ that no man maye enclose any of the wastes or Goats within the Ilande
without the vewe or lieue of the warin̄ or the Courte /

Itm̄ that no Sherisse or Bayliffe maye arrest any Tenaunte of the Lord
or carry him out of the Ilande for any Tresspas /

21

Item that no Inheritoꝛ off the Jlande maye keepe carry or lead loʃe any dogges
or curres in the heath or elʃe where, to the diʃturbance off the game
or to Dꝛiue them out off their paʃtures /

Item that no man within the Jlande may hunt any game from the firʃt daye
off Maye Anno domini vnto holyrood daye the laʃt vpon payne off xxxvijd /

Item that no man ought to erect or bincd vpp any new howʃe in the heath
or elʃe where, wthout licence off the Lord Conʃtable or his Court

Item that no mans ʃeruant ʃhall hunt within the warren but by the ouſyght
off the warynoꝛ vpon payne off xs for every tyme /

Item that no man ought to take any fiʃhe on the xꝛ alowd dayes /

Item that all fiʃher men ought to keepe their tydeꝛ with their boatꝭ and fiʃhe
vpon the ʃea coʃtes by the Cuſtome /

Item that all Jlanders ought ʃufficientlye to fence their woodeꝭ, And that they
ought to keepe out their Cattayle out off their woodes /

Item that the keperꝭ ought to apprehend and preʃent all that hauke any off
the ixꝛ Courtes or any other Court, and hedge leaveꝭ /

Item where by the wordꝭ off the Charter, viz nullus piscator emens pisces /
yt ſheweth that no fiʃhe takers be bownde to pitch their fiʃhe at the
Croſſe off Corffe, but the buyarꝭ onlye, and the fiʃhe takers to be
at libertye to carry at their pleaſure, without that lett, yet it
appeareth by the Court Rolleꝭ, that aꝭ well the takers aꝭ the buyarꝭ
haue been amerced for that default from tyme to tyme /

Item that the Warrens and Baylieffeꝭ maye arreʃt bodyly for treʃpaꝭ againʃt
the Lord off the Caʃtle aꝭ well within Corffe aꝭ without /

Item that the keperꝭ ought to bringe all ſuch Dearꝭ aꝭ they fynde Dead or
hurt to the Barbigan before the Corcnerꝭ /

finis

A bryff note off the contentꝭ off the
Newe Charter, graunted July 17, 18° Eliz, and Exemplifyed at
the Requeſt off the maioꝛ Baron & Burghers off Corfe, July 16, 19ᵗ Eliz. —

Dñs Caſtri et heꝛed ſ ht Habuint eaꝭ libertates tenſuet et comoditates
quaꝭ aliquiꝭ Conſtabul, vel Cuſtoꝭ Caſtri, ꝑꝰ hauēt habuit ꝑ conceſʃione, vel aliquoᵗ legali modo, iure, Vſu, ꝑſcriptoꝰ ſine titulo /

Curuit et Inſula de Purbeck eſtendit, in long ʼet Latit ꝓut aliquo
tempore ante Datuu ꝓſentiu conſueuit /

ficebit, Ballivo et aliis officiar' Dñi facerent ꝑ ambularent et ponere metas et Bound
quoties eis placuerit absqꝫ lře suñ alio warrant̃ /

Castr̃ Dñm de Corffe et tota Jñsula et oẽs libr̃ eorundem, tam ꝑ aqua
quam ꝑ terram sunt exempt' de officio et potestate Admirall' et
nullus Admirallus judicialiter sedebit, infra Jñsulam ꝓdc̃am /

Dñs Castri et heredes sñt admirall' et facient et exercebunt coram
se ballivñ, seu ministris, ꝑ oia que ad officñ Admirall' ꝑtinet, ꝑ
oñibus offensis, contract', et transgressionibus et ea audire et
determinare /

Dñs Castri et hered' ẽ habebunt regim' oñiuⁿ actionum et secular' ꝑ mare
vel ꝑ terram, si aliqˢ comissio fřa seu libat' finierit, in contract'
varua erit /

Dñs Castri et heredes ẽ ar sorbient et minist' corp ꝑ tempore custus'
de retro libi sñt et quiet̃ de oibus Custum Theolonij ẽ et ẽ
ꝓisñ Castri ꝑ dñi

Dñs habet custodiam Castri de Bromwicb̃ ꝑ durante vita sua /

Dñs et Deputat' sẽ heñt potestatem capiendi ministros /

Nulla ꝑsona, armatura, nec instrument bellica capiat extra Jñsulam /

Maior et habitantes Burgi de Corffe heñt omnes libertates quas
ab antiquo habuere ex comissione, usu vel ꝓscript /

Maior et Barones et inhabitantes burgi de Corffe habuit et exercebit
oẽs libertat' sñt Barones de quinqꝫ portubꝫ /

Dñes inhabitantes Jñsule de Purbecke exonerant' de ꝓ visor' hospic'
Dñi Regine /

Maior Barones et inhabitantes insule ꝓdcẽ non ponentur in aliquibꝫ Jurat'
ẽ aliquo contracta forinm insꝫ negotijs infra insulam, non ꝑtinent̃
terr̃ extra Jñsulam ẽ quibꝫ inꝣ anclar pote̶r ont debeant /

Dñs Maior, Barones et inhabitantes Jñsule ꝓdcẽ, habent oẽs libert'
ꝓdcãs, absqꝫ disturbac' Justic̃ suũ, aut alioꝝ officiar' siue ministroꝝ
dñe Regine, et sup osten' ꝓmissꝫ vol dupł eorundem sũt expedit̃
in Cancellar' Dñe Regine, coram Justic de utroqꝫ Bañ, coram
Thesaur et Baronibus de Sc̃rio, et in omnibus cur̃iis de
Record ꝑ totum Regnm Anglie /

finis

22

The Charter of March 10, 27° Eliz. adds some new Powers & Advantages to
the Office of Admiral; & Grants That S.r Christopher Hatton &c shall be
Admirals as well by Water as by Land, & upon the High Sea on the Coasts
or near the Isle of Purbeck; & in all Havens, Creeks, Rivers, Arms of the Sea &c
within the Island; & shall exercise their Jurisdiction there. And Constitutes S.t
Chr. Hatton his Heirs & Assignes, Admirals; & gives & grants to him &
them the Office of Admiral & Admiralty for ever; with all Forfeitures, Profits,
& Advantages thereunto belonging.——— Note this Charter is the same in
all other respects with that Exemplified July 16, 19° Eliz; & certainly was
granted only for the sake of these Additional Powers & Advantages———

23

STVDLANDE,

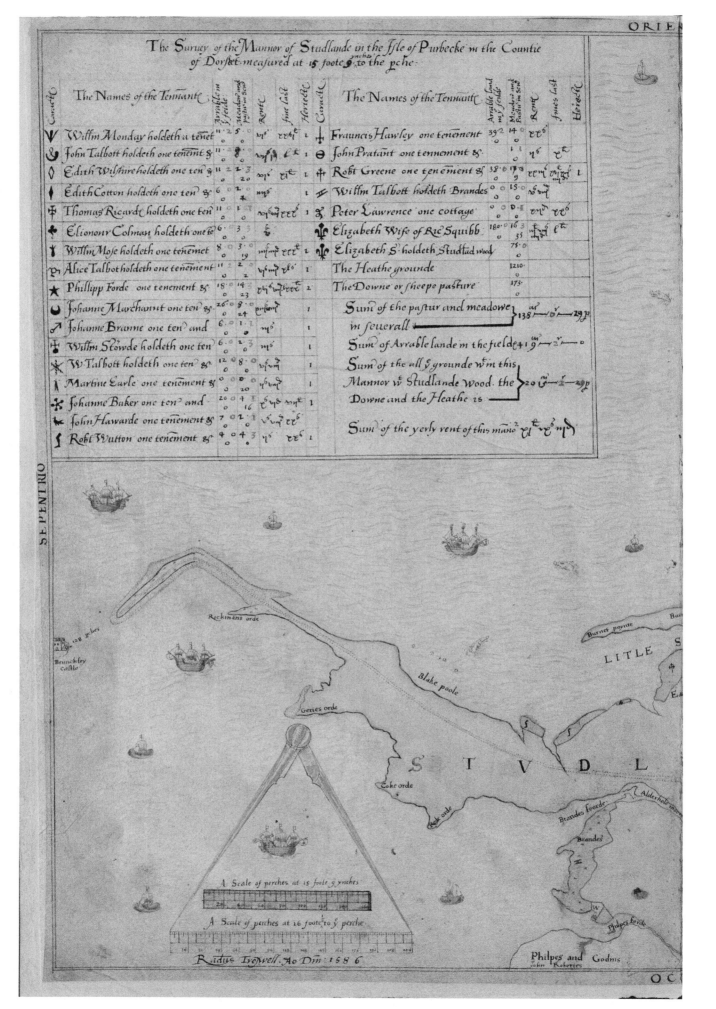

The Survey of the Mannor of Studlande in the Isle of Purbecke in the Countie
of Dorset measured at 15 foote 9 ynches to the pche

SEPTENTRIO

A Scale of perches at 15 foote 9 ynches

A Scale of perches at 16 foote to ý perche

Radus Treswell Ao Dm 1586

Philpes and Godnis
John Roberts

OC

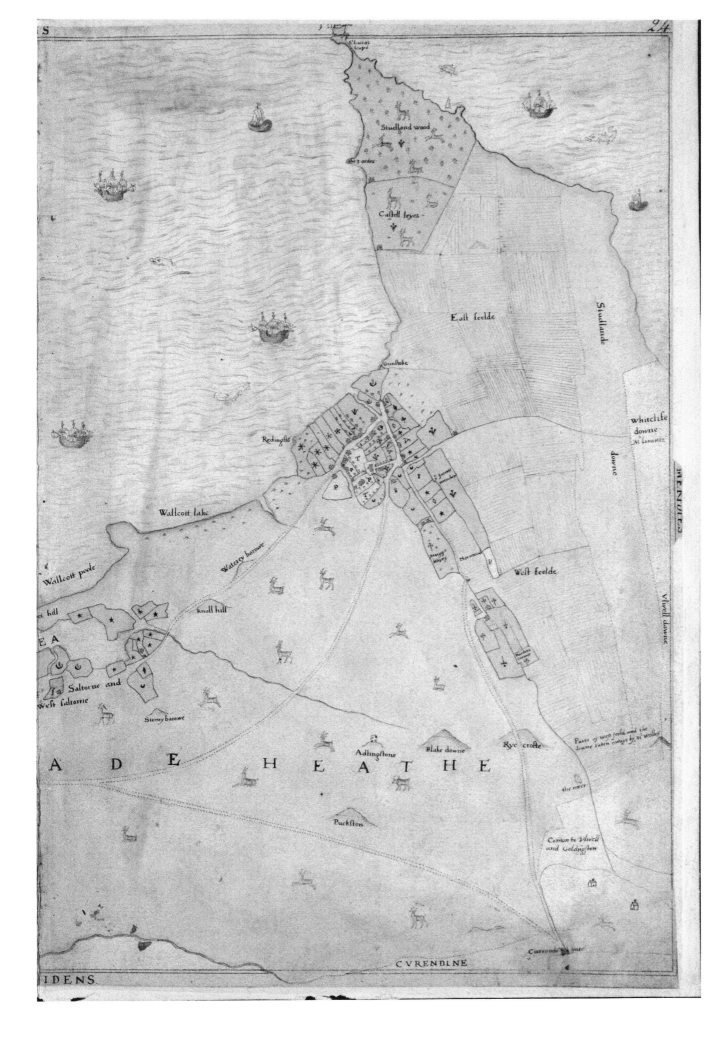

S

24

St Lucas cope

Studland wood

the 3 ordes

Castell leyes

East feelde

Studlande

Gunstole

Whitclife downe
Mr Lorance

Redingf

downe

Wallcott lake

West saltorne and

Saltorne and

Wallcott poole

hill

EA

Knoll hill

Watery barowe

S James feuender

Norman

West feelde

Viwell downe

P

Stoney barowe

Passe of west feeld and the
downe taken image by M welley

A D E

H E A T H E

Adlingstone

Blake downe

Ryc crofte

the river

Puckston

Cotton to Viwell
and Goldngston

CVRENDLNE

IDENS

The Survaye of the mannor of Studland

in the Ile of Purbecke, in the countye of Dorsett
with the Landes conteyned in the same surbayed
and measured after ys fote 9 ynges to the pole,
Anno Dm 1586.

Tennantes by Copye of Court Rolle

William Mondaye holdeth to him and Thomas his
sonne sucessiuelye by a Copye signed with the hande of
Robarte Cummy, Steward dated 6. Septemb, Anno
16. Elizabeth Regina, as followeth /.

Rent vid /	One Tenemente with a close of pasture adioyning to the same	v ad — o — o
fyne laft xxd	Of Erable Lande in the feildes	11 acr — 2 r — o
hariott. 1 /	Commo of pasture for lx sheepe vpon the Downe and heath /	lx

Jhon Talbott holdeth to him selfe, willm his
sonne and Urie his sister of the demyse of John
Dodington by coppye dated 3 July Ao 24 Elizabeth
Rgni as followeth /.

Rent /	A Tenement and a close of pasture adioyninge to the same	4 ad — o — o
ffyne laft	Two closes at Walterne late in the tenure of willm Monday	4 ad — o — o
harriot. i	Of Lande in the Common feildes	11 acr — 2 r — o
Rent for the 2 closes vid	Commo of pasture for lx sheepe vpon the Downe and heath, aforesaid	

Edith Wolshere widowe and willm her sonne
this was somtm Ant Talbott hold sucessiuelye of the demyse of John Dodington
Steward there by a Coppye dated 29 May Anno
25 Elizabeth for our Tente as followeth /.

Rent vid	One Tenement with etc /	iis — 3r — 20p
ffyne Laft ei	Of Lande in the feildes	11 acr — 2 r — o
heriott. i /	Common of pasture for lx sheepe vpon the Downe, heath aforesaid	lx

9

Edeth Cotton widowe holdeth during her
widowes estate, by coppye made to John Cotton her
husbande deceasd, dated ij. September, A° 30. Henry
8. as followeth /

Rent vijs	A Tenemente wth a close of pasture /		i — 0 — 20ᵈ
Fyne	Of Erable Lande in the feildes /		6 — 0 — 0
Heriott i	Common of pasture for xxx Sheepe on the Downe and Heath aforesaid /		xxx

       Shee holdeth more by the same Coppye

Rent ijd	A close at Salterne wth conteynes /		0 — ½ — 24 28

       Thomas Richardes holdeth for terme of his life
by coppye dated 15. Junij Anno primo Elizabeth Rne
as followeth /

Rent vijd	A Tenement wth a close of pasture /		i — 0 — 0
Fyne xvjs	More of Erable Lande in the feilde /		ij — 0 — 0
Heriott ij	Common of pasture for lx Sheepe on the Downe and Heath aforesaid /		lx

       Hee holdeth more at will /

Rent iijd	A close at Saltern wth conteyneth /		0 — ½ — 0
Fyne ijd			

       Elinore Colman holdeth duringe her widowed
by a Coppye granted to Nicholas Colman her
husbande deceasd, dated 26 Octobr Anno. 5. et 6. Phi
et Marie as followeth /

Rent xs	A tenement and 2 closes belonging to the same /		3 — ½ — 0
Fyne xvijs	More of Erable Lande in the comon feilde /		6 — 0 — 0
Heriott i	Common of pasture for xxx Sheepe as is aforesaide /		xxx

       William Mose holdeth to him selfe Johane
his wife and Maryrye their daughter suvvessiuely of
the demyse of John Bodmyton Steward there by
Coppye dated 3. July A° 29 Elizab. Rne as followeth /

Rent vijs iiijd	A Tenement wth a Crofte belonging to the same /		0 — ½ — 20ᵈ
Fyne xxs	A other close of pasture next farme meadowe /		2 — ½ — 39 23
Heriott i	Of Erable Lande in the feilde /		8 — 0 — 0
	Common of pasture for xl Sheepe as afore /		xl

Alice Talbott daughter of willm Gentill

holdeth by a Copye to willm Talbott her husband
dated 28 Octobr Anno 5 et 6 Phill: of Mar, as
followeth

Rent vijd ijf	One Tenement with a close	j li — j s — 12 d ob
ffyne xls	One Crofte against the same by the ponde	0 li — 2 s — 30 d
hariott j	Of Erable Lande in the feilde	ij li — 0 — 0
	Common of pasture for lx sheepe on the downe & heate aforesaide	li

Phillipp fforde, and John his sonne holde

Joyntsimely of the demyse of John Doding ton
steward there by copye dated 29 Octobr Anno 25
Elizabeth Rei, as followeth

Rent vijd	One tenement with a close	ijs — j s — 42 d ob
ffyne xxxs	One other close by farme meade	j s — j s — 9 d
hariott j	Of Erable Lande in the feildes	ijs — 0 — 0
	Common of pasture for lx sheepe at id aforesaid	li

They holde more by the same Copye

Rent iijs	A Cottage with a courtayne te	2 s — 0 — 10 d
	Of Erable Lande in the feildes	6 s — 0 — 0
	Common of pasture for xxx sheepe at id aforesaid	xxx s
Rent iiijs iijd	One other Tenement and three close at west Walterne	4 s — 0 — 0
Rent vs	More three close at East Walterne	5 s — j s — 0

Johane Marchaunte holdeth duringe

her widowehead of the graunte of Sr George
de La Line knight by copye dated

Rent iijd iijd	One Tenemente late willm Brymninge	0 — j s — 0
ffyne	One Close of meadowe lyeinge against the same	0 — 2 s — 30 d
hariott j	Of Erable Lande in the common feildes	ijs — 0 — 0

The same holdeth in like manner,

Rent xijd	The Cote of a Tenement	3^qu^ - 3^r^ - 14p
	Of Erable Lande in the feildes	12^cu^ - 0 - 0
Rent xijd xijd	One close of Underwood called Monthays	1^cu^ - 3^r^ - 4
	Of Erable Landes in the feildes	6^ai^ - 0 - 0
	Common of pasture for Vxx Sheepe as is aforesaide	Vxx

Shee holdeth likewise at will,

	One close of pasture at Galtorne	1^ai^ - 2^r^ - 16p

Johane Braune widowe holdeth dureing her
widowed and to Willm Brenne her sonne of the demyse
of ffrauncis Browne esquire and the Lady Anne his
wife by Coppye dated,

Rent iijs	One Tenement with a close	1^ai^ - 1^r^ - 0
Ayne	Erable Lande in the comon feildes	6^ai^ - 0 - 0
Heriott j.	Common of Pasture for xxx Sheepe as is abouesayd	xxx

William Strowde holdeth for terme of
his life of the demyse of Henry Poling esq by
coppye dated 27 July Anno 6. Elizabeth sue as
followeth

Rent iijs	One Tenement wt a close adioyning to the same	2^ai^ - 3^r^ - 0
Ayne	Of Erable Land in the feildes	6^ai^ - 0 - 0
Heriott j.	Common of pasture for xxx Sheepe vpon the downe and path aforesd	xxx

William Talbott and Richard Talbott
doe holde successiuely of the graunte of ffrauncis
Browne the Lady Anne his wife by copy dated 15
Junij Ao 6. Elizab. sue as followeth,

Rent xiijs iiijd	One Tenement wt orchard and gardein and iij closes	8^ai^ - 0 - 0
Ayne	Common of pasture for lx Sheepe as is aforesaide	lx
Heriott j.	Of Erable Lande in the feildes	12^ai^ - 0 - 0

Martin Earle and Vincent Earle
doe hold successively by Copye dated 15 Marii
Anno 14 the Elizabeth of the demyse of Henry
Hormye esquire as followeth

Rent ij s iiij d	One tenement with a yardein adioyning to the same	0 — 0 — 20
Ayne		
Heriott j		

Johane Baker widowe and Alyce Baker
her daughter holde of the demyse of Frauncis
Browne by copye dated 26 Octobr Anno
5 the Eyzet Mar as followeth

Rent xxij s	One Tenement with ij closes of pasture adioyning to the same	4 — 0 — 8
Ayne xij d	One Close adioyning to John Brabant	0 — 1 — 8
Heriott j	One Arable Lande in the feilde	2 — 0 — 0
	Common of pasture for a hundred sheepe on the downe & heath aforesaide	0

Johane Hayward holdeth for terme of her life
of the demyse of Sir Thomas Arundell knyght by
a copye dated 19 Nouembr Anno 35 of Henr 8 as
followeth

Rent iiij s iiij d	One Tenement with a close adioyning to the same	1 — 0 — 0
Ayne xx s	One Arable Lande in the common feildes	7 — 0 — 0
Heriott j	Common of pasture for xl sheepe as is abouesaide	0
Rent xij d	Also one close of pasture at Galterne	1 — 1 — 0

Robart Wotton and John Greene holde
there successiuely of the demyse of Henry Ormye
esquire by copye dated 6 Septembr Anno ii Elizabeth
Reg as followeth

Rent ij s	A onre close and one other close called Clergayte rent	4 — 3 — 0
Ayne xx s	A Tenement newly erected in the same	
Heriott j		

William Talbott and John Talbott holde
of the demyse of Margaret Russell late wyfe
of Tarent by copye dated ii May A 28 Henr 8
as followeth

Rent xx s iiij d	One Close of pasture called Brandes contayninge	15 — 0 — 0
Ayne		
Heriott j		

ffrauncis Hawley

ffrauncis Hawley holdeth at the
will off the Lord in manner and forme following
sometime the Bondl... before Eliz Cradle

Rent vii s/ iij d	Due Tenement with certeyn closes off meadow and pasture adioyninge to the same	14 li — 0 — 0
ffyne	Off erable lande in the feildes	39 a — 2 r — 0
heriott	Common off pasture for ij Sheepe as is abouesaide	dd

John Prattant

John Prattant holdeth to himselfe Henry
Shattocke and John Prattant sonne off the saide
John, off the demyst off John Dodington
steward there by copye dated 29 maij Anno 25 Eliz virtue
as followeth

Rent ij s j d	Due Tofte called Pipers hayes	1 a — 1 r — 0
ffyne xx s /3		

Robart Greene

Robart Greene holdeth for terme off
his life off the graunt off Sir John de La Zyne
knight by copye dated 14 August Anno 2 et 3 ph
et Mar as followeth

Rent xx iiij d	Due clos called mugg hayes	8 a — 1 r — 0
ffyne xxj s xiij iiij d	A Tenement with a yarde	1 a — 1 r — 0
heriott j o	Due clos called Barkers corner	1 a — 3 r — ij f
	Due clos lying at Chaltern	5 a — 3 r — 0
	Off erable lande in the feildes	38 a — 9 r — 0
	Common off pasture for ij hundred Sheepe as is abouesaide	dd

Peter Lawrence

Peter Lawrence, Gertrude his wife and
Johanne their daughter hold successively for terme
off their lives, off the demyst off John Dodington
steward there by Copye dated 29 Octobr Anno
25 Elizabeth And one peece off ground as followeth

Rent xij d	Due peece off wast ground lying at mosse wall corner	0 — j r — 0
ffyne ij s ij d		

Summe

Summe totalis xj li

Rent iiij d ffyne ij s heriott dbl by wod	Als Nightingall e Als Smithe hold during their lives one Cottage with	0 — j r — 0
Rent iiij d ffyne henss iij d heriott dbl by wod	Ric Brown e Tomasin his wife hold one Cottage during their lives And George Brown one Cottage	0 — j r — 0

29

Tenauntes by Indenture

Elizabeth wife of Richard Squibb, Stephen
within Squibb their sonne hold for terme of their lyves
of the demyse of ffrauncis Browne esq and Ladye Anne
de la Lynde his wife by Indenture dated j January Anno
primo Elizabeth as followeth.

Rent iij liij viij	The Capitoll mansion house of the Demaynes of the said manor	li 0 — 18 — xij
Ayne l	One close over against the same	l — ij — 36 xij
money 30 l xvij s	One meadowe called farme meadowe	9 — ij — 35 xij
	One close against the same	4 — j — 26 xij
	The erable lande in the feilde	180 — 0 — 0
	Commo of pasture for iiij hundred sheepe as is aboue said	li s 196 — 3 — 35

They hold more by the same lease a copyce called Medland
and castell leyes copice, wherein all the customarye Tenauntes clayme comen of
Estouers rent. | 75 — 0 — 0

The pasture for sheepe vpon the downe conteyneth | 173 — 0 — 0

The wast grounde in the heath conteyneth | 1210 — 0 — 0

The content of all the groundes within this manor ys | 2015 — x — j x

A breife note of the whole manor

Of pasture in severall	128 — iv — 38 x
Of erable lande in the feildes	419 — ij — 0
Of Meadowe	9 — ij — 31 x
Of coppice woodes	46 — 0 — 0
Sheepe pasture vpon the downes	173 — 0 — 0
Of wast groundes in the heath	1210 — 0 — 0

Sum of the whole rent of this manor ys xj li xvij s iij d

LANGTON WALLIS, and
EASTINGTŌ

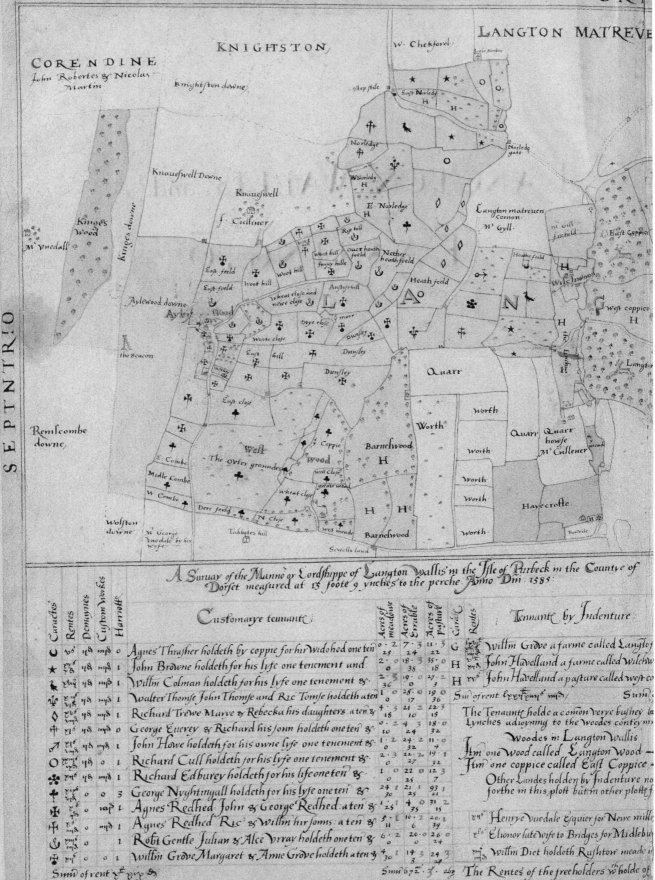

KNIGHSTON

CORENDINE
John Robertes & Nicolas Martin

Brightston downe

W. Chekforef
Litle Birline

Step stile

East Norled

Norledge

Norledg gate

W. Norledg H

Knaueswell Downe

Knaueswell

J. Culliner

E. Norledge H

Langton matreuers comon
Mr Gyll

nt Gill Ichfeld

East Coppice

Kinge's Wood

Kinges downe

Mr Vnedall

Rye hill

Ouer heath feeld

Nether heath feeld

Heathe feeld

Wilchwoo

East feeld

Woot hill

Woot hill

Woot hill

fnrycy hills

L

Anstofehill

Heath feeld

A O

N

G

West coppice

Langto

East feeld

Wheat close and newe close

moor

Dunsley

the Beacon

Aylewood downe

Ayle Wood

Woote close

Drye close

Dunsley

H

Septntrio

East hill

Dunsley

Quarr

Worth

East close

Quarr

Remfcombe downe

Worth

Quarr howse
Mr Culliner

Well Wood

Coppie

Barnefwood
H

S. Combe

The Ovter groundes

well close

greate mead

Worth

Midle Combe

W. Combe

wheat close

Worth

H

H

Hayecrofte

Wolston downe

Mr George Vnedale by his wife

Derre feeld

N Close

west meade

Worth

Bonvile

Jabbotes hill

Barnefwood

Sewells land

A Survay of the Mannor or Lordshippe of Langton wallis in the Isle of Purbeck in the Countye of Dorset measured at 13 foote 9 ynches to the perche Anno Dm 1585

Caructes	Rentes	Demaynes	Custom Workes	Harriott	Customarye tennantes	Acres of meadowe	Acres of errable	Acres of pasture	Carue	Rentes	Tennants by Indenture
C				0	Agnes Thrasher holdeth by coppie for hir widohed one ten	0	27	3	G		Willm Grove a farme called Langfo
★					John Browne holdeth for his lyfe one tenement and	2	18 3	35	H		John Havelland a farme called Wilchw
				1	Willm Colman holdeth for his lyfe one tenement	2	19	27 2	H		John Havelland a pasture called west co
				1	Walter Thomfe John Thomfe and Ric Tomfe holdeth a ten	0	26 0	19 0			Sum of rent
				1	Richard Trewe Marye & Rebecka his daughters a ten &		21 2	22 3			The Tenaunts holde a comon verye bushey la
				0	George Euerey & Richard his fonn holdeth one ten &		24	32			Lynches adioyning to the Woodes conteyn
				1	John Howe holdeth for his owne lyfe one tenement &		32	4			Woodes in Langton wallis
O			0	1	Richard Cull holdeth for his lyfe one tenement &		27	32			Item one wood called Langton Wood
				1	Richard Edburey holdeth for his life one ten &		25	7			Item one coppice called East Coppice
		0	0	3	George Nyghtingall holdeth for his lyfe one ten &		21	93			Other Landes holden by Indenture no
				1	Agnes Redhed John & George Redhed a ten &		25	21			forthe in this plott but in other plott
		0		1	Agnes Redhed Ric & Willm hir fonns a ten &		6	39			Henrye Vnedale Esquier for Newe mille
		0		1	Robt Gentle Julian & Alce Vrray holdeth one ten &		20 0	26 0			Elionor late wife to Bridges for Midlebu
		0	0	1	Willm Grove Margaret & Anne Grove holdeth a ten &		14 3	23			Willm Diet holdeth Rushton meade

Sum of rent

Item ther is belonging to fome of thes Tennantes a Shepe walke called Aylewood downe contayning 77 ... 22 ches in the wh fowre haue comon for 210 sheepe

The Rentes of the freeholders wh holde of
The extente of all the groundes wthin this Man
The rente of the hole manno Langton W

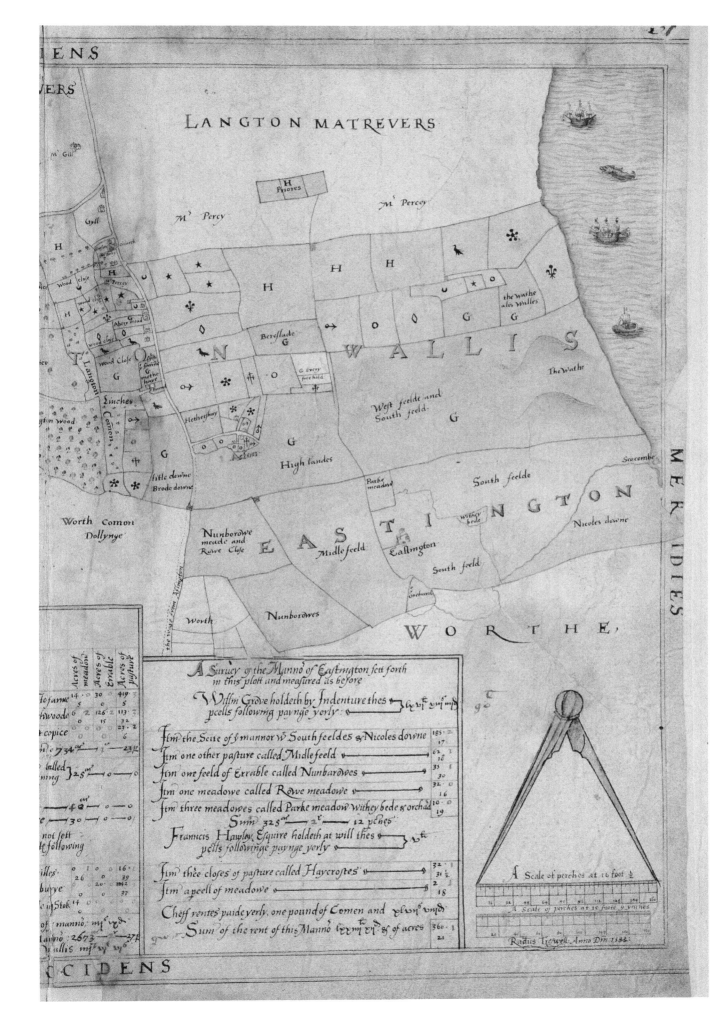

LANGTON MATREVERS

Priores

M² Percy

M⁵ Percey

Gill

Wood close

Wood close

Aber wood

Wood close

Langton

Linches Comon

ton Wood

little downe
Brode downe

Bereslade

Hethershay

Aston

High landes

Worth Comon
Dollynge

Nunborowe
meade and
Rowe Close

Worth

Nunborowes

N

WALLIS

the Wathe
alis Walles

The Wathe

West feelde and
South feeld.

Parke
meadow

EASTINGTON

Midle feeld

Eastington

South feeld

Withey
bede

South feelde

Nicoles downe

Scocombe

Orchard

WORTHE

Acres of meadow	Acres of Errable	Acres of pasture			
To Janne	14	0	30	419	3
hwoode	6	2	126	113	7
copice	0	15	23	23	2
... 734ᵉ	...	1	...	23ᵖ	
talled ning	25ᵐ	0	0	0	
...	4	0	0		
...	30	0	0		

noi sett
ft following

illes	0	0	0	16	1
...	26	20ᵉ	1042	29	
huyye	0	0	37		
...e in Stok	14				
of manno	my				
manno 2673	27ᵖ				
allis					

A Survey of the Manno of Eastington sett forth
in this plott and measured as before

W²ᵐ Grove holdeth by Indenture thes
pcells following paynge yorly:

Itm the Scite of y manno w¹ South feeldes & Nicoles downe ... 185 2 / 17

Itm one other pasture called Midle feeld ... 62 2 / 16

Itm one feeld of Errable called Nunbarowes ... 35 1 / 30

Itm one meadowe called Rowe meadowe ... 32 0 / 16

Itm three meadowes called Parke meadow Withey bede & orchad ... 10 0 / 19
      Sum 325ᵐ ... 2ᵉ ... 12 pches

Franncis Hawley Esquire holdeth at will thes
pells followinge paynge yorly ...

Itm thee closes of pasture called Haycroftes ... 32 1 / 31½

Itm a pcell of meadowe ... 2 0 / 18

Cheff rentes paide yerly, one pound of Comen and ...
      Sum of the rent of this Manno ... & of acres ... 360 3 / 21

A Scale of perches at 16 foot ½

A Scale of perches at 16 foote 9 ynches

Radius Trewell Anno Dm 1586

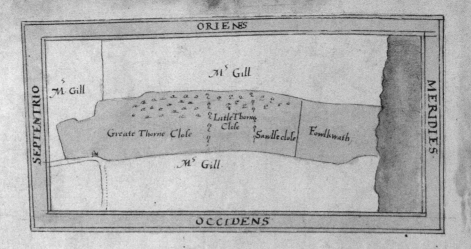

This plott contayninge these 4 percells is percell of the groundes belonging
to the capitoll house or farme of Langton Wallis, knowen by the name
of Langton farme, and now in the occupation of Willm Crone, wc closes
could not be sett in the plott of the same manner because they are almost
a myle Southward from the same farme, The content whereof
are sett downe in the terreday of Langton Wallis amongst the other
groundes, wc the saide Willm Crone holdeth. x. x.

MIDDLEBVREY

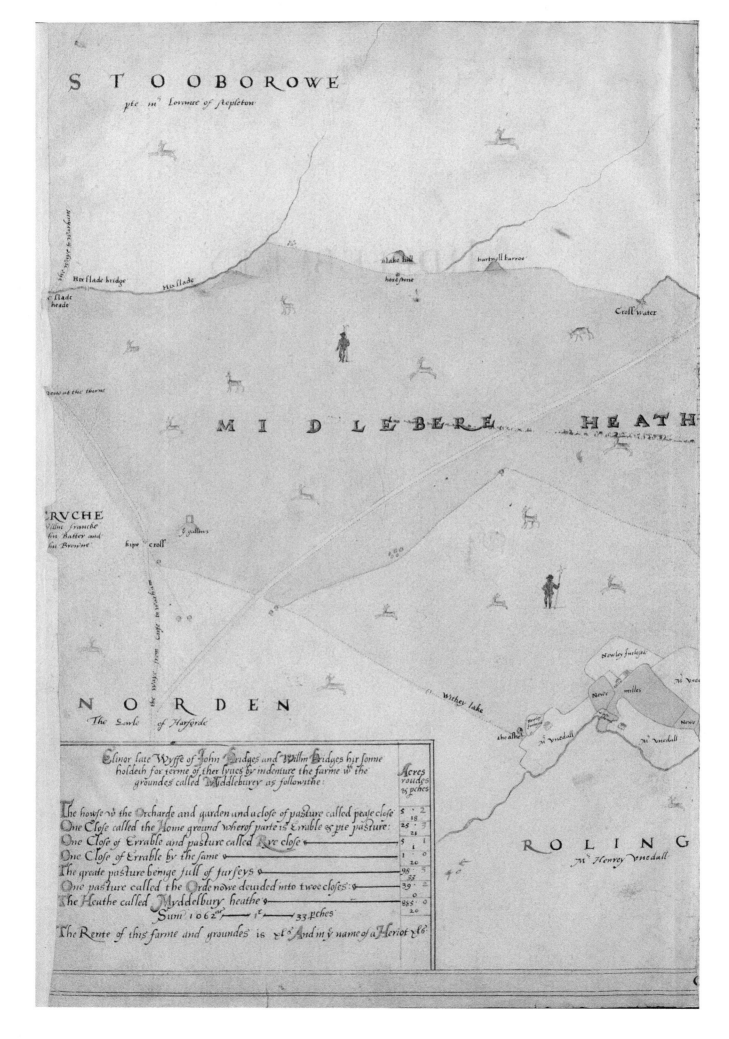

S T O O B O R O W E

pte in y Lordure of ftepleton

the waye to warham

Hir flade bridge

Hir flade

blake hill

hore ftone

hartnell barroe

Croff water

c flade heade

Rowe at the thorne

M I D L E B E R E   H E A T H

RVCHE
Willm francke
hir Batter and
his Broune

Kipe croff

y gallous

N O R D E N

The Sarle of Harforde

Withey lake

Newley Inclosed

xi Vne

Newe   milles

Henry forboro

the afhe

xi Vnedall

xi Vnedall

Newe

R O L I N G

Mr Henrey Vnedall

Elinor late Wyffe of John Bridges and Willm Bridges hir fonne
holdeth for terme of ther lyues by indenture the farme with the
groundes called Middleburey as followethe:

Acres
roudes
& pches

The howfe with the Orcharde and garden and a clofe of pasture called peafe clofe — 5 · 2 · 18

One Clofe called the Home ground wherof parte is Errable & pte pasture: — 25 · 3 · 21

One Clofe of Errable and pasture called Rye clofe — 5 · 1 · 0

One Clofe of Errable by the same — 1 · 20

The greate pasture beinge full of furfeys — 98 · 33 · 5

One pasture called the Orde nowe deuided into twoe clofes: — 39 · 0 · 2

The Heathe called Myddelbury heathe — 885 · 0 · 20

Sum 1062 ¼ — 1 ᵈ — 33 pches

The Rente of this farme and groundes is xᵈ And in y name of a Heriot xᵈ

SLEPE
the Donghters of Cadbury

34

Flokes foorde

the Weyst

is Ame

Pele cl   Pele clofe   Home grounde

Salte pitts

Rye clofe

Pasture
Pasture   Saltes   Pasture

Saltes

Mr Afheley
Mr Afheley
Orde
Orde poynt
Orde

Eafte midleburey
Mr Afheley   Orde
Saltes

Nfheleys lande

Sherfozd bridge

WICHE
Mr Yheley

TON

A Scale of perches at 15 foot 9 ynches
A Scale of perches at 16 foote and ½ to the perche

Radas Trefwell Anno Dni 1586

ORIENS

A Surey

of the mannor of Lordeshippe of Langton Wallis in the Isle of Purbecke in the in the Countie of Dorsett Suayd and measured after 15 foote & ynches to the powle or pearch in Anno domini 1586

ffreeholders

Henrye Kendall Esquier holdeth freelie to him & his heires one messuadge and certaine landes called Sherforde lyinge neut Sherforde bridge late John Sandfordes & before one Hoopers by sute of courte & what other seruice they knowe not And payeth yearely for his cheese rente at mighes } iiij d

John Clavell Esquier holdeth freely to him & his heires certaine Landes in Orcharde late purchased of Symons Darye & before one William Payned by sute of courte & what other seruice they knowe not & payeth yearly for his cheese rente at the feast aforesaide } vj d

William Culliforde gent holdeth ffreelie to him & his heires certaine landes in Quarre late purchased of William Sarrombe gent by sute of courte & what other seruice they knowe not & payeth yearely for his cheese rente at ye feaste aforesaide } i d

Nicholas Dewrey gent holdeth freely to him & his heires certaine landes in Durneforde by sute of courte and what other seruice they knowe not & payeth yearely for his cheese rente at the feast aforesaide } i d

Walter Newborough gent holdeth freelie to him & his heires certaine landes in Easte Orcharde by sute of courte & what other seruice they knowe not & paieth yearely for his cheese rente at the feaste aforesaide } ob

Robarte pmitter holdeth to him and his heires certaine landes in Burshowe late prll of the mannor of Afsrington by sute of courte & what other seruice they knowe not and payeth yearly for his cheese rente at the feast aforesaide } ob

William ffranke of Easte Oritke holdeth freely to him & his heires certaine landes in Easte Oritke by sute of courte & what other seruice they knowe not } sed nm

Henry Knedale Esquier holdeth freely to him and his heires certayne landes in newemylles some tymes John Trewes by sute of courte & what other seruice they knowe not } sed nm

Nicholas Wadham and George Tanner Esquiers holdeth freelie to them &
theire heires certaine landes in Bremestombe sometymes & regesters by sute of
Courte & what other service they knowe not _____ Sect end

John Syff gent holdeth freely to him & his heires certen landes in Langtone
Matraders by sute of Courte & what other Service they knowe not _____ Sect end

Sum tibi Contrib — iiij li ix d

36

Customye tenntes

Agnes Thressher widdowe late the wife of George Thressher
Decessed holdeth Duringe her widdohed according to y customte
of the manner of the Demised of Anne Willoughby one
Tenemente which Contayneth as followeth

Item A Tenamente and A small medowe adioyning to the same ———— 0 —— 2ᵛ —— 25 p
Item one close erable Against the same. ———— 3ᵃˣ —— 0 —— 33 p
Item two Closes of pasture called woode close ———— 5ᵃˣ —— 2ᵛ —— 23 p
Item one close of erable amonge the groundes nere the sea side ———— 4ᵃˣ —— 2ᵛ —— 31 p
Item A close of pasture devided in 2 closes adioyning to y lynche, called
heage feelde ———— 6ᵃˣ —— 0 —— 39 p

20ᵃˣ —— 1ᵛ —— 31 p

The same Agnes Thressher payeth for her yearely rennte x d and for
A prell of the Demaued holden at will ij d and for customworkes iiij
The fine payde at the taking of this farme xiij s iiij d

The reuerron of the p'misses is graunted vnto John Coxe Cecely Coxe
the Daughter of Peter Coxe and Alice Charitie the Daughter of
Williame Charitie, & nomt pmit Cotagij Durid ptm modo in tennris
Agnet Thressher vid. Durant vidictal is by a coppie subscribed by S'
Frauncis Willoughby knight & William Growe Dated xxiiij Septemb
Anno Rne Elizabeth p'sone Tenemente w y lands by y tenh & farmed vt sapra

John Browne of the age of 6 x yeares holdeth for
his owne life these parselles followinge

Item the howse w'th woodclose and the groundes adioyning to the same ———— 6ᵃˣ —— 3ᵛ —— 39 p
Item ij furscy closes of pasture foyning our Orkines groundes. ———— 12ᵃˣ —— 1ᵛ —— 1 p
Item ij closes of pasture nere norlege gate ———— 8ᵃˣ —— 1ᵛ —— 24
Item iiij closes of erable Against his howse ———— 17ᵃˣ —— 2ᵛ —— 0
Item ij closes of pasture at stepe stile ———— 9ᵃˣ —— 1ᵛ —— 34 p
Item A close of erable nere the sea side ———— 1ᵃˣ —— 1ᵛ —— 38 p

56ᵃˣ —— 0 —— 16 p

The same John Browne payeth for his yearely rente xx s x d And for
a prell of the Demaued holden at will ij d and for custom workes iiij
The fine payde at the taking of his farme xxxvj

William Colmann of the age of 57 yeares holdeth for his life these percells ffollowinge

		a		r		
Item the howse and two meddowes		2		3		36 p
Item i. close of pasture by the commony		3		1		32 p
Item i. close of pasture againste the langton farme		11		2		29 p
Item A close of pasture by the lynge		9		2		20 p
Item A close of pasture by the sea side		13		1		36 p
Item A close of pasture at steepe stile		8		1		6 p
		49		1		39 p

hariet i

The same William Colmann payeth for his yearly rente xviij and for a parcell of Demanes holden at will ij and for custome workes iiij The fine paide at the takinge of the farme xx vj

Walter Thowse holdeth to him to John his sonne and Richarde Thowse, the sonne of Robarte Thowse for terme of there lynes Successinely by Acoppie Sealed and Subscribed by the saide william Broue Stewarde Dated xxiiij Septembris Anno Rne Elizabeth xvij whirh bontayneth

Item the howse wth the ground Adioyninge to the same		3		0		0
Item ij. Close of pasture called heath feelde		9		2		38 p
Item i. Close of pasture called norlege		7		1		38 p
Item ij. Closes of erable against his howse		11		3		29 p
Item i. Close next the sea side		14		0		28 p
		46		1		13 p

hariet i

The same Walter Thowse payeth for his yearly rente xx iij and for a parcell of the demanes holden at will ij and for custome workes iiij The fine paide at the takinge of his farme Lt

Richarde Trewe holdeth to him to Marye and Reberta for tearme of there lynes Successinely by Acoppie of the Demyse of Sr ffraunces willinghbye knight and Subscribed by William Broue Steward Dated xxiiij Septembris Anno Rne Elizabetha xvij whirh tobayneth One tenamente viz

Item the Tennament wth A prcell of meadow		1		3		17 p
Item A close of pasture called wodde close		2		3		9 p
Item ij closes of pasture shouting one langton matrevers comoy		8		1		24 p
Item A close against the howse erable		10		0		0
Item A close of erable amongs the groundes by the sea side		11		2		9 p
Item ij Closes of meddowe adioyning to langton matrevers comoy		3		0		1 p
Item one other greate close of pasture		11		2		22 p
		49		1		3 p

37

The same Richarde Treve payeth for his yearely rente xs viij
and for a percell of the Demanes holden at will ij d for custome
Workes iiij d The fine paide at the takinge of his farme — xs

George

George holdeth to him to Richarde
his sonne and Elizabeth his Daughter for terme
of there lyves Sutcessively of the demise of the
Lady Anne Willoughby widowe by a coppie sealed
the seale and subscribed by Sr ffrauncs willoughby
knight Henry willoughby Essquier Robarte Demundocke
Stewarde and Richarde Taverner Reever Dated
xxj die Marij Ao xxvij Regis Henr viij on vollage

Containeth

Item the howse and Crofte		0	2r	10 p
Item one close of erable shontinge one langtoy conioys bnode downe	3ar	0	24 p
Item a close of pasture shontinge one Walter Thoms heath feelde	7ar	1r	16 p
Item ij closes of pasture Callede norledts	10ar	3r	16 p
Item a close adioyninge to Bereslade	1ar	3r	0
	23ar	2r	26 p

The same George Everye payeth for his yearly rente xj s and
for a percell of the Demayned holden at will ij d and for custome
Workes iiij d the fine paide at the takinge of his farme xx s

John

John Howe of the Age of 45 yeares holdeth
to him selfe deuring his life as ffolloweth

Item the tenement wt a crofte		0	2r	4 p
Item A close by the same	1ar	2r	0
Item A close against the howse	0	1r	30 p
Item A close of pasture shontinge one Langtoy meat rente to conioy	16ar	0	10 p
Item one close of erable adioyninge to Langtoy conioy	2ar	0	32 p
Item one close adioyninge to bereslade	13	0	0 p
Item A close of Erable against the pound	9ar	2r	0
	37ar	0	36 p

The same John Howe payeth for his yearely rent xj s viij d
for A percell of the Demaynes holden at will ij d for custome
workes iiij d the fine paide at the takinge of his farme xx s

Richarde

Richarde holdeth for terme of his life
as followeth

Item the howse wth a partell of medowe ———————————— 1^{ar} | 2^r | 0

Item one other Close by the same ———————————— 1^{ar} | 1^r | 0

Item one Close of trable shoutting one herslad ———————————— 7^{ar} | 2^r | 25 p

Item one Close of trable shoutting one Langtoy tonnoy ———————————— 3^{ar} | 0 | 14 p

Item one Close of pasture called heath feeld ———————————— 9^{ar} | 0 | 0

Item one Close of pasture shoutting one watrenerd Connoy ———————————— 10^{ar} | 1^r | 32 p

Item A Close of trable next the sea side ———————————— 1^{ar} | 1^r | 38 p

Item one other close of trable lyinge betweene howse & tren ———————————— 10^{ar} | 1^r | 3 p

44^{ar} | 3^r | 19 p

The same Richarde Cutt payeth for his yearely Rente xxiij^s iiij^d
and for a partell of Demayned ij^d y fine paide at the takinge of y farme xl^s

hariet i / Reue vj^s

Richarde Edberie holdeth for
Terme of his Life as followeth :/

Item the howse and ij closes of pasture ———————————— 3^{ar} | 1^r | 20 p

Item ij Closes of pasture adioyninge one worth tonnoy & Langtoy tonnoy 4^{ar} | 0 | 15 p

Item one close against the howse ———————————— 6^{ar} | 3^r | 0

Item one close neere the sea side ———————————— 15^{ar} | 1^r | 25 p

Item one close of pasture shoutinge on Gulls heath feeld ———————————— 6^{ar} | 1^r | 12 p

35^{ar} | 3^r | 32 p

The same Richarde Edberie payeth for his yearely Rente vij^s and
for A partell of the Demaynes he holdeth at will ij^d and for custom
worked iiij^d The fine paide at the takinge of the farme vj^{li} viij^d

hariett i / Reue vj^s viij^d

George Nightingall holdeth
Duringe his life as followeth)

Item the howse wth garden orcharde & y great medowe adioyninge to the same 7^{ar} | 2^r | 20 p

Item the proost medowe ———————————— 4^{ar} | 0 | 6 p

Item A medowe called well close ———————————— 2^{ar} | 2^r | 6 p

Item A close of pasture called whete close ———————————— 7^{ar} | 1^r | 13 p

Item A close of trable called north close ———————————— 3^{ar} | 3^r | 36 p

Item A close of pasture called deere feeld ———————————— 2^{ar} | 2^r | 0

Item A pasture called the ropitt ———————————— 13^{ar} | 2^r | 18 p

Item one pasture called Cast close wth the crier ground & medowes 63^{ar} | 1^r | 133 p

Item iij Closes of trable called Caste tombe, west tombe & midle tombe 14^{ar} | 2^r | 10 p

Item one Close of pasture called norleden ———————————— 10^{ar} | 0 | 0

129^{ar} | 2 | 22 p

12 g^{ar} 2 rt 22 pes

The same George Nightingall payeth for his yearely rente xx^s vij^d the fine paid at
takinge of the farme xxx^{li} vj^s viij^d

hariett iij / Rent lll vj^s viij^d

38

Agnes Redhed late the wife of Thomas Redhed deceassd.
holdeth during her widdowhed accordinge to the Custome of
the mannor, the Remaynder thereof to John Redhed and
George Redhade sonnes of the said Thomas for terme of their
lyves successively by A Coppie subscribed by Sr Ffrauncis
Willoughby knight Robarte Henwudocke Rigard master
Servayors & Steward of the mannor, one tenemente
in Ayshwade Cawled wester Bargaine dated xxvij Septembris
Anno Secundo Regis Edwardie Sexti wch contayneth as folle

Item A tenemente called the wester Bargaine and A close ——— 1ᵃᶜ 3ʳ 28p
Item A close of Arrable Againste the same ——— 1ᵃᶜ 2ʳ 0
Item A close called wester Gill ——— 4ᵃᶜ 3ʳ 22p
Item A close called weste hey feelde ——— 3ᵃᶜ 3ʳ 9p
Item one close of pasture cawled wester Dimsley ——— 13ᵃᶜ 3ʳ 13p
Item A meddow cawled brode meade ——— 1ᵃᶜ 1ʳ 25p
Item one Close cawled wott Gill ——— 3ᵃᶜ 2ʳ 16p
Item one Close of pasture cawled Fursie Hills ——— 3ᵃᶜ 2ʳ 1p
Item one Close of Arrable shouting out ayshwad Downe ——— 2ᵃᶜ 2ʳ 35p

— 37ᵃᶜ 0 35p

The same Agnes Redhede payeth for her yearly kente xᵈ
for Custome worke iiijᵈ the fine payde at the takinge of the same

Comony for 50 Sheepe one Ayshwad Downe

The saide Agnes houldeth during her widdowhead one
other tenemente in Ashywade cawled the Easter bargaine
the Remaynder thereof to Rigarde Redhead & william
Redhed two other of the sonnes of the saide Thomas for
terme of their lyves Interessvely by A Coppie
subscribed by the saide Sr Ffrauncis willoughby
knight and william Browne dated xxvij Septembris
Anno xᵐᵒ Elizabeth wch contayneth as followeth

Item the tenemente wt garden and Orchard ——— 0 2ʳ 20p
Item one close of Arable by the same ——— 10ᵃᶜ 2ʳ 6p
Item A medow cawled the little meade ——— 3ᵃᶜ 0 6p
Item ij closes of pasture Cast Gill ——— 9ᵃᶜ 0 34p
Item a pecell of meadot in the same ——— 1ᵃᶜ 1ʳ 0
Item one close of pasture devided into ij closes cawled Dimsley ——— 7ᵃᶜ 3ʳ 36p
Item one close of pasture called watt Gill ——— 2ᵃᶜ 2ʳ 29p
Item A pecell of meddowe called watt Gill mead ——— 1ᵃᶜ 0 15p

— 36ᵃᶜ 1ʳ 16p

The same Agnes Redhed payeth for her yearly Rente x s iiij d
and for custome workes iiij d ffine paide at the taking of the farme xx s

Commoned for 50 sheepe one Alwood downe /

Robarte Sentle holdeth to him to Julyan Errate
And Mirt Errate Daughters of Robarte Errate
for therme of there lyves Successiuely by a copie
sealed and subscribed by Fraunces willoughbie
knight and subscribed by William Crowe dated
die mercurij xxbo die Aprill Anno Regni Elizabeth
undecimo One tenemente which contaynth as folowth

Item the tenamente with orchard & garden	o	2 r	16 p
Item one close of Erable nere the same	2 ar	o	10 p
Item A meddowe by the same	3 ar	2 r	o
Item one close of Erable called Easte feelde	9 ar	i o	8 p
Item one meadow called woot hill meade	o	3 r	10 p
Item one close of pasture called woot hill	5 ar	3 r	116 p
Item ij closes called nere close & white close	7 ar	3 r	8 p
Item A meadow called Rise meade	i ar	o	2 p
Item one close of Erable called Rise hill	3 ar	2 r	34 p
Item one close of pasture called over heath feelde	4 ar	3 r	10 p
Item nether heath feelde w 2 prtts of meadow	12 ar	2 r	24 p
Item A close of Erable called mett gate	o	3 r	16 p
	52 ar	2 r	29 p

The same Robarte Sentle payth for his yearly Rente xiij s iiij d
ffine payde at the takinge of the farme xxvi s viij d

Commoy for 80 sheepe one Alwood downe /

William Crowe thonger holdeth to him to margaret
Crowe the Daughter of william Crowe brother of the /
saide William Crowe thonger and Anne the Daughter
of Dauyde Crowe an other brother of the saide williame
for terme of there lyves Successiuely by a copie sealed
and subscribed by the saide Fraunces willoughbye /
knight & subscribed by William Crowe steward
Dated die Jouis undecimo die Octobris Anno Regni Elizabeth
xiij one Tenamente which contaynth as folowth

39

Item the tenemente with gardey _____ 0 — 1r — 14p

Item the medowe against the same _____ 0 — 3r — 30p

Item a close of pasture called woott close _____ 5a — 0 — 10p

Item a close of pasture called drye close _____ 4a — 2r — 0

Item the medowe by the same _____ 3a — 2r — 0

Item a pasture called dursley _____ 3a — 2r — 14p

Item a rusey medowe beneathe the same _____ 3a — 1r — 39p

Item one close of earable called Ote hill _____ 5a — 1r — 3p

Item one close of earable called Ester feilde _____ 9a — 2r — 0

Item one close of pasture called Austond hill _____ 7a — 3r — 30p

44a — 0 — 20p

The same William Growe payeth for his yearely rente vij li. ll

Common of pasture for 70 sheepe one Ashywood Downe

Somme of the Acres in the tenures of y Custonary tennantes 672a — 3r — 26p

Somme totalled of the rent of Custonary tennants x li x s d

The Customary Tennantes holdeth adioynannte to the woods a troy
of pasture beinge a verye bushey grounde called Lynches alles langboy
Common which contayneth by measure 25a — 0 — 0

The Customarye Tennantes hold there A shippe walke which
extendeth from Kingesdowne into allwood groundes & contayneth by
measure 77 — 1r — 22p

There is within this manor one woode called Langtony
woode which contayneth by measure 40a — 0 — 0

Also one other Coppice called the Easte Coppice which
Contayneth by Measure / 30a — 0 — 0

Tennentes by Indenture:

William Brode holdeth by Indenture dated
of   all the Cottage and farme
house of Langtony Wallis late in the occupation
of John Samways gent contayning these pcells following

	a	r	p
Item the farme house wth A meadowe called meathaye	3	0	27
Item one close sometyme ij closes called wood close	16	1	0
Item one pasture called litle downe	20	1	4
Item A meadowe called Hethexsey	5	2	10
Item the greate pasture called west feeld & Broade Downe	18	3	35
Item A pasture called the wallis	11	1	24
Item A close of Erable nexte the same	12	1	2
Item A close of pasture called Higge landes beinge pte of west feeld	67	2	39
Item A meadowe called A brehaye	1	3	8
Item A meadowe in Sandwich by the bridge called Franck meade	2	0	0
Item the winter pasture of A meadowe in Sandwich	1	2	0
Item one pasture sometime iiij closes called greate thorne			
Little thorne Sandles close and forekvate	96	1	3
Item A close of pasture called Bernstade	12	1	24

The same William Brode payeth for his yearly rente by vj li viij s iiij d

465	3	10

Item the saide William Brode hath also common of Pasture
wth his Rother beastes according to his tenure in the wood called
Langtony Woode

John Havelande gent holdeth by Indenture
to him and Thomas his sonn for terme of there
lyves the farme called wilkesrodde also wilkeswoode

	a	r	p
Item the house wth garden Orcharde & meadowe by the same	6	0	0
Item the Lynges beinge Pasture and meddowe wth the pondes	16	3	17
Item ij closes of pasture and meadowe of ye demayne lying ont ye backe of ye psonage	15	1	19
Item ij closes of pasture called worleades	9	2	18
Item A meadowe next m payes house	1	1	8
Item 3 closes of Erable called proyers	9	0	0
Item i close of erable & ij of pasture adioyninge to m pereys his grounde	73	2	15
Item A pcell of grounde in Haycrosse wth A cottage	0	2	0
Item A pcell of grounde wth a cottage called lytle Byndon	0	0	16
Item A close of Erable & pasture called wester worles & easter worleys	7	2	28
Item iij pastures caled Barnswoode	56	2	4
Item in axorth feldes	29	0	2
Item east Langton fellde	14	0	0
Item A meadowe at the east ende of the Lynges	2	2	0

247	0	7

The same John Havellande payeth for his yearly rent ~ ix d

The fine paide at the takinge of the farme ~ v s

The same John Havellande holdeth by lease for 21 yeares
Dated the 6. of Julij in the xxvj yeare of the Ma tie Raigne a pasture ~ 23 m ~ 2 r ~ 6 p
called the west Copice rent

The same John Havellande payeth for his yearely rent ~ xx s

The fine paide at the takinge of the farme ~ v s

Henry Snedale esquier Edmond Snedall
and John Snedale his sonnes holdeth for terme of
theire lyves by Indenture ye pasture caled newe milled
as followeth

Item iij Closes of pasture ~ 16 a[i] ~ 1 r ~ 39 p
Item of meadowe the moytie of ij plotes ~ 0 ~ 1 r ~ 26 p

16 m	3 r	25 p

The same Henry Snedall Esquier payeth for his yearely
Rente ~ vij s

Elinor Late wife to John Bridges &
William Briges her sonne holdeth for
tearme of theire lives by Indenture the
farme with the groundes called middlebury

Item the howse with Orchearde and Garden ~ 0 ~ 3 r ~ 0 p
Item A close called pease close Erable ~ 4 m ~ 13 r ~ 18 p
Item the home grounde whereof partie is Erable ~ 25 m ~ 13 r ~ 21 p
Item a close called wie close the one halfe Earrable the other pasture ~ 5 a[i] ~ 1 r ~ 1 p
Item the greate pasture ground beinge fursie ~ 98 m ~ 3 r ~ 35 p
Item a close by the same of Erable ~ 1 m ~ 0 ~ 20 p
Item A pasture called the odd ~ 15 a[i] ~ 1 r ~ 38 p
Item one other pasture called the odd with the salted ~ 24 m ~ 0 ~ 2 p

177 m	1 r	13 p

There is also belonging to this farme, a heath called middlebury
heath and Langtony heath with contayneth ~ 885 m ~ 0 ~ 20 p

The same Elinor payeth for here yearely rente xij s the fine
paide at the takinge of the farme ~ lxx s

The same Heath aforesaide belonging to the mannor of Langton and farme of mudelberye is bonded as followeth from mydelberye house to ffloke forde from ffloked forde to neither Crosse water, from neither Crosse water to Owtcrose water from Owtcrose water, to Herstone from Herstone to a Hiphill of Stones from thence to Hutslyde bridge from thence to Hutslade head from thence to Type Crosse from thence one furlonge unto tire thorne from thence to horethorne from thence to mythe lake and they kepte the lake to Charsforde Bridge whirh contayneth in all by measure as Aforesaid

William Dyet holdeth for terme of his life by Indenture dated the xxth daie of Marche Anno xxxvjo of the raigne of kinge Henry the viij by the graunte of Dame Anne Willoughbye of woadlande in the Countie of Dorsett

Item one pcell of meadow lyinge and beinge in Langton meade _____ in the pishe of stoke   14 —— o —— o past

The same William Dyet payeth for his yearely rennt viij iiijd   Sum of Acres The fine paide at the taking of the farme —— iijli vjd   in this Manno

Sum Totalis of the tenaunts by Indenture lxxjli xvjs vmd   2673 xs ijd

The whole rente of this manno of Langton wallis iijxxli vijs viijd

The custome of the mannor of Langton Wallys by the Othes of the Tenaunts.

Inprimis where but one life is in possession the lorde And here liuethe in fee Royo Also that the wife of every Customary tenante duinge possessed of any Customary Tenannte shall haue her widdowe estate in the same And every customary tenaunte except the Cottagis and widowes shalle paie A herritt at his deathe Also that every Tenante maye make a Quarrey for Tyle stone in his grounde paying to the lorde for every lode thereof one penney And that the lorde maye keepe as well a lete as a Courte Baron vpon the mannor, and that the liberties incidente to the same Lete extendeth ouer all the groundes apperteyninge to the manno and that all waysses strayed Treasure Trouye goodes and Cattells of fellons & fugitiues are incidente to the Lorde of the same manno And that the purchaser may Surrender the Reuersioners estate so that the Reuersioners doe paie noe parte of the fine And that the Tenaunts of Langton wallis haue alwaies digged turues in langton hoath adioyninge vnto mudelbery heath wch turuoy is bounded by A way in the north side of the gallowse from the porte waye easte vnto thorne moore

The Survey

the manno of Eastington in the Isle of purbecke iiij only of Dorset the plot whereof is sett forth in the plott of Langton wallis and measured at 15 foote ix ynches to the yerde in Anno domini. 1586.

Ffree holders

William Chaldott gent holdeth freely to him and to his heires certen Landed and tenements in East kimbridge called Chaldotts Landes by knighte service and payeth _____ xxvjd

William Cyferwast gent holdeth freely to him in the right of his wife late wife to Thomas Darkombe gent certaine Landes in Quarre iiij in other places next course by knightes service and payeth _____ xvijd

Hugh Sheverell Esquier holdeth freely to him and his heires certaine Landes and tenements called kimeridge late Thomas Arneys by knightes service and payeth yearely _____ iiijs iiijd

John Clavell Esquier holdeth freely certaine Landes in Little Kimridge by knightes service and payeth yearlie _____ xxd

The same John Clavell holdeth freely to him and to his heires certaine Landes called smedmore by knightes service & payeth yearely _____ viijd

The same Jo: Clavell holdeth of Alfrington freely of Soueraigne Ladie the Queene by knightes service & payeth yearthe _____ ijs

The same John Clavell holdeth certaine Landes and tenements in Langton late George Gerrod gent and late Robarte Rawlines by knightes service & payeth yearlye viij iiij and payeth at his death in ye name of harriott. xxd and for releve viij iiij and payeth yearly _____ xiijs iiijd

John Sandesforde holdeth one close neere Corff Castell called Eye Close by knightes service and payeth yearely _____ j libr

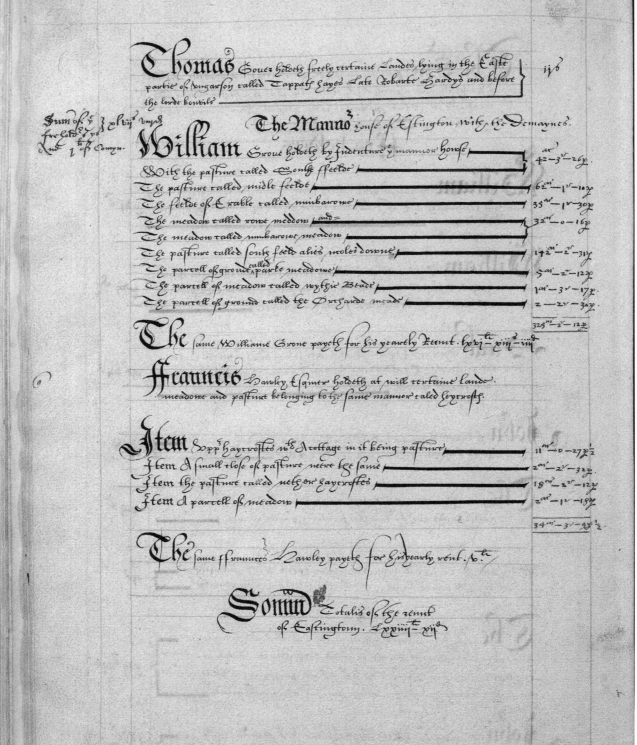

Thomas Gouer holdeth freely certaine Landes lying in the Easte
partie of Longansor called Tappals Hayes late Robarte Hardys and before
the lorde Bonvils _____ ij li

Sum of þe freeholders yt hold & at 1ly Comen

The Mannor house of Estington with the Demaynes

William Grout holdeth by Indenture þe mannor howse _____ a li — iij s — xxvj d

With the pasture called Sonth ffeelde _____ vj li — j s — x d

The pasture called midle feelde _____ xxxv a — j s — xxx d

The feelde of Erable called mukarome _____ xxxij a — o — xvj d

The meadow called rovst meddow and =

The meadow called mukarome meadow _____

The pasture called Sonth feele alias molet downe _____ xvij a — ij s — xxj d

The parcell of ground called parte meadowe _____ v a — ij s — xxij d

The parcell of meadow called vythie Blade _____ j a — iij s — xvij d

The parcell of ground called the Orchard meade _____ ij — ij s — xxx d

xxv a — ij s — xij d

The same William Grout payeth for his yearly Rent. lxvj li — viij s — iiij d

ffrauncis Hawley, Esquier holdeth at will certaine landes
meadowe and pasture belonging to the same mannor caled Heyrosth.

Item one Heyrosth with A cottage in it being pasture _____ xj a — o — xxvij d ob

Item A small close of pasture neere the same _____ ij a — ij s — xxij d

Item the pasture called nether Hayrosth _____ xvij a — ij s — xij d

Item A parcell of meadow _____ ij a — j s — xviij d

xxxiiij a — iij s — xxj d ob

The same ffrauncis Hawley payeth for his yearly rent. v li

Somma Totalis of the rent
of Estington. lxxvij li — vij s

The Snave of the manno' of Affrington all's Aldrington in the Isle of Purbucke in the Countie of Dorsett with the groundes belonging to the same

Free holders

William Darcombe gent holdeth freely certaine landes in Burshewe and the mill called Afflett mylt & paieth yearly   xx^s

John Clavell Esquier holdeth freely certaine landes in Orchande and payeth yearly therefore   vij^s

Henry Bonvile holdeth freely certaine landes in ye manner of Affrington and payeth yearly   lk of pep.

George Snedall gent holdeth freely in the right of his wife certaine landes in Woulgarston and payeth yearly   ij^s

Leonard Attye holdeth freely certaine landes in Affrington & payeth yearly   viij^d

John Seward holdeth freely certaine landes in Woulgarston & payeth yearly   xvij^d

William Darcombe holdeth freely certaine landes in Woulgaston & payeth   xvij^d

George Snedall gent holdeth freely certaine landes in Woulgurston and payeth yearly   vj^d

Allyn Frampton holdeth freely certaine landes in pimphorne called Hedley & payeth yearlye.   v^s

John Wadham Esquier holdeth freely certaine landes in Woulgarston & payeth   xvij^d

Sum xxxj^s j^d and halfe a pound of peper

Ffranncis

Ffranncis Hardy Esquier holdeth at will the
moitie of the sight of the mannor & the moytie of
all the demaynes some time in the tenner of Robarte
Dollinge the elder & also the sixt parte of the same
Site & demane Landes as ffolloweth &c

Item the Site of the howse with Orchard and pondes ———————— 2^a — 0 — 33½
Item the one halfe of A pasture called Heath feilde ———————— 17^m — 3^r — 37½
Item A pasture called Easte Heath feilde ———————— 22^a — 1^r — 4½
Item A pasture called Haytroftes ———————— 26^a — 2^r — 24½
Item A pasture called new leeyed ———————— 15^a — 1^r — 6½
Item A meadowe called Gaustones ———————— 1^a — 3^r — 9½
Item A meadowe wch hath byne devided in to manie pceles called
East meade ———————— 10^a — 0 — 0
Item A pcell of meadowe adioyning to Sholde ———————— 1^a — 1^r — 0½
Item A close called Bulled close ———————— 2^a — 3^r — 10½
Item A pasture called Timberlands ———————— 4^a — 1^r — 20½
Item A pasture called Butesbroughe ———————— 14^a — 0 — 28½
Item A pasture called Crofts ———————— 5^a — 0 — 35½
Item A pasture called west feilde ———————— 5^a — 2^r — 20½
Item A feilde of Erable called north east feilde ———————— 43^a — 0 — 15½
Item A feilde called north west feilde ———————— 53 — 3^r — 34½
Item A pcell of Erable called Sheepe gayes ———————— 7^a — 2^r — 32½
Item A one other feilde Adioyning to north ———————— 45^a — 1^r — 15
Item A parte of A meade called west meade ———————— 4^a — 3^r — 8½
Item A parcell of ground wood called Affringley grove ———————— 5^a — 0 — 0
Item a pcell of meadowe wheron standeth a Tenement decayed ———————— 2 — 3 — 30½

                                                                            292½ — 2^r — 8½

The same Ffranncis Hardy payeth for the moyety
of the site of the mannor & the moyetie of all ye demaines p pm xij^d

The same Ffranncis Hardy for ye sixte pte of the Site
and Demaynes keepes A plough for the nesessarye service
At the castell of the Lorde from time to tyme

Robarte Dollinge oR Corfe holdethe
During the lyves oR his father & him selfe
By the graunte oR Robarte Hardie sone
time Lorde oR the same manno these pcells
Followinge

Item A meadowe called Dowe close meadowe ——————— 2ᵃ — 0 — 10ᵈ
Item A close oR pasture called Dowe close ——————— 7ᵃ — 0 — 29ᵈ
Item one other small meadowe called Dowe close meadowe ——— 2ᵃ — 0 — 10ᵈ

                                                  11ᵃ — 1ᵛ — 9ᵈ

Elizabeth Hobbes late wife oR Robarte
Hardie holdeth for terme of her life this pcell following

Item A close oR pasture called greate Dypshelo ——————— 7ᵃ — 0 — 0
Item A parte oR A meade called west meade ——————— 3ᵃ — 3ᵛ — 30ᵈ
Item A nother close oR pasture called little dipshelo ——————— 3ᵃ — 1ᵛ — 36ᵈ
Item the moyetie or one halfe oR heath feelde ——————— 17ᵃ — 3ᵛ — 37ᵈ
Item A close called weste feelde ——————— 5ᵃ — 2ᵛ — 17ᵈ
Item One close adioyninge to kingstoy ——————— 33ᵃ — 3ᵛ — 3ᵈ

                                                  71ᵃ — 3ᵛ — 3ᵈ

Sum of the whole rent
oR this manno is xxxxli xvs ijd ob j

A Breife note off whole rent
off the mannors and landes aforesaid.

The rent and Revenewes off the Castle off Corfe yb — xx.li viij.s viij.d

The rent off the mannor off Studland. yb — xj.li ix.s iiij.d

The rent off the mannor off Langton Wallys. yb — iiij.xx vj.li vj.d

The rent off the mannor off Estington yb — iij.xx xij.li xiij.d

The rent off the mannors off Aflington yb — xxx.li xxj.s

Sum totallis off all the rent
within the Jsle off Purbecke. — vj.c xxbj.li vij.d viij.d

Whereof {
To be payd at our Ladye day — vj.vij.li v.s iiij.d
And at Mighelmas ————— vj.xx.li xix.s
}

The rent off the Landes at wareham withowt the Jsle yb — x.li vij.d

The fee off the Baylywyke off waymouth, Melt, Gallwell, Portland
and wareham, together with the hundredb off Ranbarowe Ruthmore
and Haseller by yeare. — vj.li

Sum totallis off all the Rent and
Revenewes with the fee off the Baylywork
aforesaid yb ————— vj.c xliij.li ij.d viij.d

TRANSCRIPT OF THE SURVEY

[Folio 12r]

The survey of the manor of Corfe with the castle called Corfe Castle in the Isle of Purbeck in the county of Dorsett, with the honours, lands, rights, customs, and services belonging to the same made in the year of Our Lord 1586.

Freeholders

The mayor of Corfe holds the passage of wool and cheese through the whole Isle for the which he pays yearly to the lord of of the Castle two pounds of wax price 12 d. at the feast of St Michael the Archangel [29th September]	2 lbs of wax price 12 d.
William Dacombe, gentleman, holds one close of pasture late the land of the parson of Corfe containing 1 acre called Toleys Crose and pays yearly one pound of wax price 6 d. at the feast aforesaid	1 lb of wax price 6 d.
Robert Dollinge, in free socage, one burgage late Richard Phillips and pays yearly therefor at the feast aforesaid	3 d.
Henry Uvedall, esquire, holds freely in socage certain lands and tenements in Corffe Castell and pays yearly at the feast aforesaid	12 d.
The same Henry holds certain lands and tenements in Radlington alias Rollingtonn to him and his heirs and pays yearly twenty horse shoes of iron at the feast aforesaid	20 horseshoes of iron, price 20 d.

[Folio 12v]

The same Henry and John Sanforde hold a certain water course leading to the mill called Brode mill and pay therefor yearly twenty sexternes of ale, every sexterne containing twenty gallons price 6 s. 8 d. at the election of the constable at the feast aforesaid	20 sexternes of ale price 6 s. 8 d.
John Trewe holds freely certain lands and tenements called North Castell within the borough of Corfe and pays therefor yearly at the feast aforesaid	4 s.

The same John holds another close in the west parts of the close of Henry Bonvile there late Richard Knights and pays yearly at the feast aforesaid	½ lb of cumin price 2 d.
Henry Bonvill holds freely one close of pasture containing 2 acres lying besides the bridge called St. Edwardes bridge and pays yearly at the feast aforesaid	½ lb of cumin price 2 d.
John Hayword hold freely one burgage late Steven Haywarde and pays yearly therefor at the feast aforesaid two horseshoes of iron with nails, price	2 horseshoes of iron price 2 d.
John Robarts in the right of Mary his wife holds freely one burgage in Corfe late Thomas Kigell father of the said Mary and pays yearly 6 d. and also he holds certain lands and tenements called Clevell and pays yearly at the feast aforesaid 2 s. 6 d.	3 s.

[Folio 13r]

William Daccombe, gentleman, holds freely one close of meadow called Piper Crofte containing three acres and pays yearly at the feast aforesaid	2 s.
John Sanforde holds freely one close of pasture called Longe Wall and pays yearly at the feast aforesaid	15 d.
John Tye holds freely one burgage and one close called Vycarys Haye and pays yearly at the feast aforesaid	8 d.
Henry Bonvile holds freely one shop late Cookes and pays therefor yearly at the feast aforesaid	2 d.
The same Henry holds freely three burgages in Corfe and pays yearly at the feast aforesaid	16 d.
Thomas Atye holds freely one burgage in West Streete and pays yearly at the feast aforesaid	2 d.
Robert Permiter holds freely one shop late Thomas Hoopers and pays therefore yearly at the feast aforesaid	2 d.
Henry Welles in the right of Mary his wife daughter and heir of John Pole holds freely one burgage with the appurtenances late Bormans and pays yearly at the feast aforesaid	3 d.

[Folio 13v]

John Barron holds freely certain lands and burgages and pays yearly 2 d. and 1 lb of wax price 6 d. at the feast aforesaid	2 d. and 1 lb of wax price 6 d.

[total] 8*d.*

William Trewe holds freely a certain parcel of land called Horse Mans Ground late Richard Whittles and pays yearly	2 *d.*

The tenements of Norden in the parish of Corfe pay yearly at Michaelmas by ancient custom twenty horse shoes of iron with nails now appraised at	20 horseshoes of iron, price 20*d.*

The tenants of the manor of Ower in the parish of Corfe pay yearly for 60 horseshoes of iron with nails of ancient custom as appears in the customary	60 horseshoes of iron with nails price 5*s.*

Sum 28*s.* 9*d.*   2 lb of wax
                   1 lb of cumin   3*s.* 4*d.*
                   1 lb of pepper[1]

[Folio 14r]

Tenants at will

The bailiff of the borough of Corfe for the time being by virtue of his office holds one meadow called Holwiche Mead containing 7 acres and pays yearly at the feast of St Michael the Archangel	7 a., o r., o p. 8*s.*

The same bailiff for the time being holds the pasture of one close called Gosse Hame containing two acres and pays yearly therefor	2 a., o r., o p. 3*s.*

John Haywarde of Newton holds at will a certain parcel of land and pays therefor yearly two bushels of salt price 12*d.* and three hens price 6*d.*	18*d.*

Sum 12*s.* 6*d.*

Tenants by copy of court roll

John Hayward holds one tenement with a cottage and diverse closes and parcels of land hereafter follows with the appurtenances in Newton in the parish of Studland together with a licence to take birds or fowl as well in the lord's commons as upon the coasts or river of the sea there and pays therefore yearly	14*s.* and one heriot

[Folio 14v]

John Hayward:

The house with the orchard and one parcel of ground called Withie Beade	4 a., 2 r., 8 p.

---

1   No pepper in the text, but 2 lb of cumin not 1 lb.

One close of pasture called Weste Heye and Winters Haye	8 a., o r., 19 p.
One other close of pasture called Easte Haye	4 a., 3 r., 19 p.
One other close of pasture adjoining to the same called Clewelsheye	5 a., 1 r., 8 p.
One other close on the west side the same called Clewelsheye	4 a., 3 r., 8 p.
Another close of arable in the same	2 a., 3 r., 33 p.
One close of arable adjoining upon Clewelsheye	2 a., 1 r., o p.
One other close lying next the same called Shannor Poynte	2 a., o r., 18 p.
One close called Dignelshaye	3 a., 3 r., o p.
The heath called Newton Heathe with the parcel of ground called Grove	682 a., o r., o p.
One close of arable called South Close	5 a., o r., 1 p.

724 a., o r., 4 p.

Richard Tuppe holds one tenement with diverse closes and parcels
of land in Ulwell in the parish of Sanwich with common of pasture
upon Ulwell Downe and Whitly Downe for sheep without number
with the appurtenances late in the tenure of Thomas Leyde and
pays therefore yearly.

23s. 4d.
and heriot

One tenement with a curtilage, garden, orchard and croft and Beane Close.	3 a., 3 r., 25 p.
One close called Ridge acre	3 a., 1 r., 24½ p.
One close called Gille Combe	2 a., 2 r., 29 p.
One close called Gille Haye	o a., 2 r., 20 p.
One close called Whitleyes	1 a., o r., o p.
One close called Touthills by Touthills land	1 a., o r., 20 p.
Four closes called new closes, and a little close	19 a., o r., 36 p.
One close called Brome Hill	3 a., 3 r., 21 p.

[Folio 15r]

One close of meadow called Brooke Meadowe	1 a., 1 r., 12 p.
One close of meadow called Mill Haye	o a., 3 r., 15 p.
With common of pasture on Ulwell Downe and Whitleys Downe for beasts without number.	

35 a., 3 r., 24½ p.

Sum 37s. 4d.

Tenants by Deed

William Newman of Poole by the assignation of John Moyle,
esquire, holds by Letters Patent for term of certain years yet
enduring all the demesne lands of the Castell or Lordship of
Corfe aforesaid and also one grist mill in Corfe aforesaid and also
all houses, buildings, dove houses, orchards, gardens, waters,
water courses, fishings and all other profits, commodities and

emoluments to the said mill belonging with the appurtenances
and pays yearly therefore   £7 13s. 4d.

One close of meadow called Moore Meadow	5 a., 0 r., 10 p.
One other parcel of meadow called Porters Meadow	1 a., 0 r., 0 p.
One close of pasture called Whete Close	7 a., 0 r., 0 p.
One close of arable called Mill Close	2 a., 0 r., 0 p.
One close of pasture called Castle Close or Castele Leyes	59 a., 0 r., 0 p.
One close of pasture called Castle Downe	46 a., 0 r., 0 p.
One close of pasture called Castle Burough	4 a., 2 r., 0 p.
And all that mill aforesaid	
Sum 124 a., 2 r., 10 p.	

John Uvedall, gentleman, holds for term of years yet enduring one
burgage in the town of Corfe with a curtilage adjoining containing
by estimation half an acre with the appurtenances late in the tenure
of Thomas Browne and pays yearly therefore   5s.

[Folio 15v]

William Grove holds the pasture of three score sheep upon Kings   36 a., 2 r., 36 p.
Woode Downe unto the lord's wood called Kings Woode, annexed
parcel of the lord's demesnes and pays therefore yearly   2s.

The bailiff of Corfe yields for eight acres of arable ground lying   8 a., 0 r., 0 p.
in the common field of Corfe called the Weste Hawes late
purchased of John Samforde and pays yearly   40s.

Henry Durrante holds the moiety of one grist mill at Ulwell and
pays therefore yearly   6s. 8d.

Thomas Crasse holds to him, Anne his wife and William their son   0 a., 0 r., 30 p.
for term of their lives a certain parcel of land called the Ham
containing by estimation 30 perches and pays yearly   16d.
The house is disused and is now converted into the orchard

The wood called Kinges Woode set forth in Langton Wallis plot
Contains   39 a., 2 r., 36 p.
        Sum: £10 8s. 4d.

Money due and payable to the Castell of Corfe yearly by the inhabitants of the Isle of
Purbeck to be collected by the Governors of the said Isle with certain hay, hens, salt and corn as follows:

The tithing of Herston	12d.
The tithing of Whitclyffe	12d.
The tithing of Langton Wallis	12d.

[Folio 16r]

The tithing of Worth	12 d.
The tithing of Afflington	12 d.
The tithing of Rollington	12 d.
The tithing of Burshewe	12 d.
The tithing of Remscombe	12 d.
The tithing of Bradlie Farm	12 d.
The tithing of one tenement in Weste Orcharde of the inheritance of John Clavell esquire now in the occupation of John Goulde	4 d.
The tithing of one tenement of William Chalcottes, gentleman, in West Orchard	4 d.
The tithing of one tenement in Weste Orcharde aforesaid lately purchased by John Clavell esquire of Simon Davye	4 d.
The tithing of Knowle	2 s.
The tithing of Easte Critch	12 d.
The tithing of Engalstone	12 d.
The tithing of Easte Tynehame	12 d.
The tithing of Weste Tynehame	12 d.
The tithing of Povingtonn	2 s.
Goldstone parcel of the tithing of Afflingtone	12 d.
Sum 19 s.	

Fodder Hay

Godlingstone for one load of hay called fodder hay	2 s.
The tithing of Herston a load of hay or 2 s.	2 s.
William Kingemann for his lands in Newton, a load of hay or 2 s.	2 s.
The tenants of the lands called Wooddeheade a load of hay 2 s.	2 s.
Sum 8 s.	

[Folio 16v]

Hens

Godlingston for the price of 2 hens	4 d.
Phitworth for the price of 6 hens	12 d.
Philpes in the fearne for the price of 2 hens	4 d.
Sum 20 d.	

Salt

Godlingston for the price of two bushels of salt	12 d.
Phitworth for the price of 6 bushels of salt	3 s.
Philpes in the fearne for the price of 2 bushels of salt	12 d.
Meddlebery for the price of 2 quarters of salt	8 s.
Sum 13 s.	

Wheat

The farm of Langton Wallis of wheat	9 bsh

The farm of Lutton of wheat	13 bsh
The farm of Worth of wheat	13 bsh
Sum 35 bushels	

[Folio 17r]

Money paid to the Castell towards the ranger and keeper's wages

Povington	25 s.
Worth	30 s.
Langton Wallis	23 s.
Godlingstone, for money called Guttor Sylver	2 s.
Sum £4	

Warehame, without the Isle of Purbecke

Francis Hawlie esquire for the meadows there by the year (18 a.)	£8
Christopher Anketel esquire for a close called Castle Close yearly	
at Michaelmas (1 a., 2 r.)	10 s.
John Rounde for one garden at Michaelmas	6 s.
Frances Gerrard for one garden at Millane as before	2 s. 4 d.
William Lane one garden by the parsonage house of St Martin's	
yearly	12 d.
John Arney one garden at Millane yearly	18 d.
John Rodgers one garden at Mighells Lane yearly	16 d.
George Gerarde for one garden at Alhallou Well yearly	12 d.
Nicholas Gerrarde for one garden at Butsherde	18 d.
The same Nicholas for one other garden called Croked Garden	
Alhalowell	3 s.
The same for another garden by Harvies house in Westreete	
adjoining to the parsonage of St Michell	4 d.
The fishing of the north river and south river there in the 28th	
year of Elizabeth's reign	28 s.
The fee of the Baylyweke of Wayemouth, Wyke, Hellwell	£6
Portland, and Warhame together with the hundreds of	
Ramburouge, Rusmore and Haseller each year	
Sum £16 16 s.	

[Folio 19r]

The abridgement of certain liberties pertaining to the Castle of Corffe in the Isle of Purbecke in the county of Dorsett contained in the old charter of the said castle, with the bounds of the Island.

The boundaries of the same Island go and do extend from a way lying between Flowersberye and a wood called Whitwaye, and from there to Ludgforde, and from there to Warehame bridge and so still from there by the sea side toward the east to a place called Studland Castle, and so from there continually by the sea coasts to St Aldomes chapel and so still by the sea coasts westward until you come to the said place of Flowresberye aforesaid.

Item that the whole Island is a warren and appertains to the Castle.

Item that all pleas of vert venison and wrecks of the sea appertains to the Castle and determinable by the constable and his steward and the fines thereof pertain to the constable.

Item, that all strangers as well of the warren as elsewhere, being attached within the bounds of the Island for any trespass done shall have justice and answer before the constable and in no other courts.

Item, if any of the town of Corffe do complain to the constable or mayor of Corffe upon any dwelling within the warren aforesaid, either for debts or other offence, the same ought to be attached by warreners, sworn, and come and answer at the next hundred court of Corffe before the constable and in no other court and the constable shall have the amercements.

Item, that the lord of the Castle shall have the one moiety of all causes pertaining to the bishop or archbishop, within the whole parish of Corffe, and the bishop's or archbishop's officers coming thither to hear causes or matters shall see their greyhounds run at the hare by the view of the warreners.

Item, if there be carts within the town of Corffe able to carry a whole tun of wine, the owners of the carts shall carry for the constable yearly, from Warehame to the Castle, two tuns of wine, and the carriers hall have for every tun's carriage 4 d. and his corrody honourable.

[Folio 19v]

Item, that the men of Corffe ought to receive certain prisoners sent to the Castle by the King's commandment at Warhame bridge, and so with the constable's aid carry them to the Castle, and when they shall be sent again to any other prison, they shall bring them again to the same bridge with the like aid.

Item, if any war happen near the Castle, the tenants of the town aforesaid by the tenure of their land ought to be in the Castle by the space of forty days at their own proper costs for the defence of the same Castle.

Item, that the tenants of the town of Corffe shall find one cart every Saturday to carry for the constable bread and beer from Wareham to Corffe and the drivers of the cart shall have their corrody of the constable or else 3 d.

Item, that the constable shall take the assize of ale, that is to say 12 gallons of ale for 3 d. as well within the town as without through the whole warren, so that the one half be of the best and the other of the second sort.

Item, that no merchant buying fish within the warren shall carry the same fish out of the said warren but that he pitch the same first at the cross of Corffe tarrying there to sell the same by the space of an hour and making default and taken flying shall lose his fish at the constable's pleasure.

Item, at the change of every constable the warrener shall summon 4 men of every of the tithings of Brunccksey and Owre to come to Corffe before the constable there in full court, to be sworn neither to convey out, nor bring into the warren any hunters or other evil doers.

Item, that no owners of any woods within the warren may cut or carry away any of their woods without the oversight of the warreners but in this order if they ask leave of the warrener and can not obtain leave then they must come to the Castle gate with witness of some of the town's men declaring the same to the porter and ask leave. And that done and approved they shall be discharged if they happen to be attached.

Item, that the constable time out of man's remembrance has had the priceage of wine of every ship arriving upon the sea coasts of Purbeck if the ship there do tarry and do stay her self with cords and anchors in the right of the lord of the Castle.

[Folio 20r]

Item, that the constable time out of mind has had the wrecks of the sea through his whole bailiwick when they happened.

Item, that the lord has had time out of mind all regal or head fishes as *graspes* [a whale or dolphin], porpoises and sturgeon taken upon the sea coasts of Purbeck.

Item, that the lord has had all falcons eyrieing [nesting, from *eyrie*] or breeding upon the bailiwick aforesaid but the constable is accustomed to reward the takers of the said fishes and falcons.

Liberties of the town of Corffe

Item, that the whole town of Corffe appertains to the Castle, and the tenants of the same town are called barons, and are as free as the barons of the five ports , but they can hold no pleas but of piepowders but all their presentments and terminations are before the constable and his steward with the amercements coming of the same.

Item, that the court of Corffe ought not to be kept but from four weeks to four weeks, except the Queen's writ happen to come.

Item, to the town of Corffe belong all judicial assigns *pola* and *bellum* and all pleas which appertain to the King and dignity of his Crown. So that the same be determined there before the King's justices.

Item, that by the common assent the inheritors of Corffe do yearly choose among themselves at the lawday held for the town at the feast Saint Michael the Archangel a mayor, two coroners, one beadle and two ale tasters.

The Customs of the town of Corffe

Item, the mayor of Corffe has used to hunt by custom the deer or any other game yearly upon May Day, accompanied with his brethren the masters of the town, inheritors of the Island and other gentlemen of the country which shall happen to come in all places of the south side of the Castle and Great Downe.

Item, that the mayor of Corffe has had by the custom yearly, and the whole year, one horse to go and depasture in the Castle ground for the service of the prince as it is thought.

Item, that the free barons and inheritors of Corffe ought to dig and have turves though the whole warren, without the denial of any person, and that they ought to drive their cattle to Holme Mount in the west walk on Whit Sunday yearly there to depasture that day and three days following.

[Folio 20v]

Certain customs and orders belonging to the Castle to be approved by the court rolls and common use.

Item, there appertains to the Castle of Corffe two lawdays yearly to be kept at the Castle gate called the out Lawdays, being of the nature of a wood court, or swanimote court, the one kept at the feast of St Michael the Archangel, the other at the feast of the Annunciation of Our Lady [25 March], at which appear all the freeholders of the Island and all the tithingmen of all the two hundreds of Roughbarrow and Hasillor with their posts and sidesmen, some with five, four, three or two as appears by records.

Item, there are two usual lawdays for the town kept at the terms and place aforesaid by the constable officer.

Item, the constable officer and steward may keep every four weeks a court called hundred court wherein are tried writs of right, pleas of trespass and debt, and all other common pleas, and at their courts be made presentments of offenders against the game and of *vert* and wreck by the rangers and warreners of Purbeck as well in the lawdays, wherein the warrener is the officer to execute process and to present all measure, weights and brewers, and other offences.

Item, every fisherman within the Island, at every lawday pays to the Castle, for licence to fish, for every boat 4*d.*, and the tithingman presents the boats of every tithing and all manner wrecks and deodands [forfeited goods] happening within their several tithings.

These customs need no proof for that they are in daily use.

Other customs and orders approved by the court rolls.

Item, that no islander ought to marry his daughter out of the Island without licence of the lord constable or other officer.

Item that no inhabitants of the island shall make any stone wall, hedge or ditch above the assize that is no higher than that a hind with her calf may easily leap over at all places.

Item, that no man ought to take or hunt any coneys, hare, fox or pheasants with dogs, nets or ferrets within the warren without licence or view of the warrener.

Item, that no man may enclose any of the wastes or heath within the Island without the view or licence of the warrener or the Court.

Item, that no sheriff or bailiff may arrest any tenant of the lord or carry him out of the Island for any trespass.

[Folio 21r]

Item, that no inheritor of the Island may keep, carry or let loose any dogs or curs in the heath or elsewhere to the disturbance of the game or to drive them out of their pastures.

Item, that no man within the Island may hunt any game from the first day of May unto Holy Rood Day [14 September] the last upon pain of 6*s.* 8*d..*

Item, that no man ought to erect or build up any new houses in the heath or elsewhere without licence of the lord constable or the Court.

Item, that no man's servant shall hunt within the warren but by the oversight of the warreners upon pain of 10s. for every time.

Item, that no man ought to take any fish on the Sabbath Day.

Item, that all the fishermen ought to keep their tides with their boats and fish upon the sea coasts by the custom.

Item, that all islanders ought sufficiently to fence their woods. And that they ought to keep out their cattle out of their woods.

Item, that the keepers ought to apprehend and present all that *harrle* [overturn?] any of the nine coverts or any other covert and hedge tears.

Item, where by the words of the Charter viz: *nullus piscator emens pisces* [No fisherman selling fish] it seems that no fish takers be bound to pitch their fish at the Cross of Corffe, but the buyers only, and the fish takers to be at liberty to carry at their pleasure without that let, yet it appears by the court rolls that as well the takers as the buyers have been amerced for that default from time to time.

Item, that the warreners and bailiffs may arrest bodily for trespass against the lord of the Castle as well within Corffe as without.

Item, that the keepers ought to bring all such deer as they find dead or hurt to the Barbigan before the coroners.

The End

A brief note of the contents of the new charter granted July 17, 18th Elizabeth [1576] and exemplified at the request of the mayor, barons and inhabitants of Corfe July 16, 19th Elizabeth [1577].

[*Italic text translated from Latin*]

The lord of the castle and his heirs shall have the customary privileges and profits which the constable or warden of the aforesaid castle have previously had from a grant or any lawful means, by right of law claimed by time or title.

The circumference of the Isle of Purbeck extends in length and breadth as it did at any time before the date of the present document.

[Folio 21v]

The bailiff and any of the lord's officers shall be allowed to carry out a perambulation and set the metes and bounds whenever they wish without a writ or other warrant.

The lord's castle and manor of Corffe and the whole Island and all of its customary privileges, both on water and on land, are exempt from the office and authority of the Admiral and no Admiral shall sit as a judge within the aforesaid Island.

The lord of the Castle and his heirs are Admirals, in person or through their bailiffs or ministers, and shall do and carry out all things that pertain to the office of Admiral, to hear and judge all offences contracts and transgressions.

The lord of the Castle and his heirs shall have knowledge of any actions and suits by sea as well as by land. If some commission is made or is delivered contrary to this charter it shall be void.

The lord of the Castle and his heirs and servants and ministers, whoever they are at the time, are henceforth free and quit from all customs, tolls, etc. for the provision of the aforesaid Castle.

The lord has custody of the Castle at Brounckseye during his life.

The lord and his deputies have the power to take musters.

No person shall take armour or an instrument of war outside the Island.

The mayor and inhabitants of the borough of Corffe shall have all the liberties which they have anciently held by grant or created by lapse of time.

The mayor, barons and inhabitants of the parish of Corffe have all the liberties and exemptions as the barons of the five ports (i.e. the Cinque Ports).

All of the inhabitants of the Isle of Purbeck are exonerated from the requirement to provide hospitality to the Lady Queen.

The mayor, barons and inhabitants of the aforesaid Island shall not be obliged to serve in any jury concerned with any legal action other than with the Island affairs, unless they hold land outside the Island for which they can or should be impanelled.

The lord, mayor, barons and inhabitants of the aforesaid Island have these aforesaid liberties, without disturbance from any justice, sheriff, or other officer or minister of the Lady Queen. Upon demonstration of the present document, or a duplicate they are exonerated (from any such disturbance of their rights) in the lady Queen's Chancery, before the justices of both benches, before the Treasury and the Barons of the Exchequer and all of the Courts of Record in the whole realm of England.

The End.

[Folio 22r]

[In a later hand]
The charter of March 10, 27th Elizabeth [1585] adds some new powers and advantages to the office of Admiral; and grants that Sir Christopher Hatton etc. shall be admirals as well by water as by land, and upon the high sea on the coasts or near the Isle of Purbeck; and in all havens, creeks, rivers, arms of the sea etc. within the Island; and shall exercise their jurisdiction there. And constitutes Sir Christopher Hatton, his heirs and assigns , admirals; and gives and grants to him and them the office of Admiral and admiralty for ever; with all forfeitures, profits and advantages thereunto belonging. Note: this charter is the same in all other respects with that exemplified July 16, 19th Elizabeth; and certainly was granted only for the sake of of these additional powers and advantages.

[Folio 26r]

The Survey of the Manor of Studlande in the Isle of Purbecke in the county of Dorsett with the lands contained in the same surveyed and measured after 15 foot and 9 inches to the pole, in the year of Our Lord 1586.

Tenants by copy of court roll:

William Mondaye holds to him and Thomas his son successively by a copy signed with the hand of Robert Smyth, steward, dated 6 September in the year 16th Queen Elizabeth [1574], as follows:

One tenement with a close of pasture adjoining to the same	5 a., 0 r., 0 p.
Of arable land in the fields	11 a., 2 r., 0 p.
Common of pasture for 60 sheep upon the Downe and heath	60
Rent 6s., fine last £26, heriot 1.	

John Talbott holds to himself, William his son and Urie his sister, of the demise of John Dodington by copy dated 3rd July year 24th Queen Elizabeth [1582] as follows:

A tenement and a close of pasture adjoining to the same	4 a., 0 r., 0 p.
Two closes at Salterne late in the tenure of William Mondaye	4 a., 0 r., 0 p.
Of land in the common fields	11a., 2 r., 0 p.
Common of pasture for 60 sheep upon the Downe and heath aforesaid	
Rent 5s. 1d. fine last £50, heriot 1, rent for the two closes 2s.	

Edith Wylshere, widow, and William her son hold successively of the demise of John Dodington, steward there, by a copy dated 29 May year 25th Queen Elizabeth [1583], one tenement as follows (this was sometime Anthony Talbot's):

One tenement with, etc.	2 a., 3 r., 20 p.
Of land in the fields	11 a., 2 r., 0 p.
Common of pasture for 60 sheep upon the down and heath aforesaid	
Rent 6s., fine last £11, heriot 1.	

[Folio 26v]

Edith Cotton, widow, holds during her widow's estate, by copy made to John Cotton her husband deceased, dated 2 September year 30th Henry VIII [1538] as follows:

One tenement with a close of pasture	1 a., 0 r., 20 p.
Of arable land in the fields	6 a., 0 r., 0 p.
Common of pasture for 30 sheep on the down and heath aforesaid.	
Rent 3s., fine [blank], heriot 1.	

She holds more by the same copy:

One close at Salterne which contains	0 a., 3 r., 24 p.
Rent 12s.	

Thomas Richardes holds for term of his life by copy dated 15 June year 1st Queen Elizabeth [1559] as follows:

One tenement with a close of pasture	4 a., o r., o p.
More of arable land in the field	11 a., o r., op.
Common of pasture for 60 sheep on the down and heath aforesaid	60

Rent 6s., fine 30s., heriot 1.

He holds more at will:

One close at Saltern which contains	o a., 1 r., o p.

Rent 8d., fine 5s.

Eleanor Colman holds during her widowhood, by a copy granted to Nicholas Colman her husband deceased, dated 26 October year 5th and 6th Philip and Mary [1558] as follows:

One tenement and two closes belonging to the same	3 a., 3 r., o p.
More of arable land in the common fields	6 a., o r., o p.
Common of pasture for 30 sheep as is aforesaid	30

Rent 5s., fine 13s. 4d., heriot 1.

William Mose holds to himself, Joan his wife and Margery their daughter successively of the demise of John Dodington, steward there, by copy dated 3 July year 24th Queen Elizabeth [1582], as follows:

One tenement with a croft belonging to the same	o a., 2 r., 20 p.
One other close of pasture next Farme Meadowe	2 a., 1 r., 39 p.
Of arable land in the fields	8 a., o r., o p.
Common of pasture for 40 sheep as aforesaid	40

Rent 4s. 4d., fine £30, heriot 1

[Folio 27r]

Alice Talbott, daughter of William Gentill, holds by a copy to William Talbott, her husband, dated 28 October years 5 and 6 Philip and Mary [1558] as follows:

One tenement with a close	1 a., 1 r., 12 p.
One croft against the same by the pound	o a., 2 r., 30 p.
Of arable land in the fields	11 a., o r., o p.
Common of pasture for 40 sheep on the down and heath aforesaid	40

Rent 6s. 4d., fine 40s., heriot 1

Phillipp Forde and John, his son, hold successively of the demise of John Dodington, steward there, by copy dated 29 October year 25th of Queen Elizabeth [1583] as follows:

One tenement with a close	2 a., 1 r., 4 p.
One other close by Farme Meade	1 a., 1 r., 9 p.
Of arable land in the fields	12 a., o r., o p.
Common of pasture for 60 sheep as is aforesaid	60

Rent 6s., fine £80, heriot 1

They hold more by the same copy:

A cottage which contains	2 a., o r., 10 p.
Rent 3s.	
Of arable lands in the fields	6 a., o r., o p.
Common of pasture for 30 sheep as is aforesaid	30
One other tenement and three closes at West Salterne	4 a., o r., o p.
Rent 2s. 8d.	
More, three closes at East Saltern	5 a., 1 r., o p.
Rent 5s.	

Joan Marchaunte holds during her widowhood of the grant of Sir George de la Line, knight, by copy dated [blank]:

One tenement late William Brynning	o a., 1 r., o p.
One close of meadow lying against the same	o a., 2 r., 30 p.
Of arable land in the common fields	8 a., o r., o p.
Rent 4s. 4d., fine [blank], heriot 1	

[Folio 27v]

The same holds in like manner:

The toft of a tenement	3 a., 3 r., 14 p.
Rent 6s.	
Of arable land in the fields	12 a., o r., o p.
One close of underwood called Monthays	1 a., 3 r., 4 p.
Rent 3s. 4d.	
Of arable lands in the fields	6 a., o r.., o p.
Common of pasture for 130 sheep as is aforesaid	130

She holds likewise at will

One close of pasture at Saltern	1 a., 2 r., 16 p.

Joan Branne, widow, holds during her widowhood and to William Brenne her son of the demise of Francis Browne esquire and the Lady Anne his wife by copy dated [blank]

One tenement with a close	1 a., 1 r., o p.
Arable land in the common fields	6 a., o r., o p.
Common of pasture for 30 sheep as is above said	30
Rent 3s., fine [blank], heriot 1.	

William Strowde holds for term of his life, of the demise of Henry Goring esquire by copy dated 27 July year 6th Queen Elizabeth [1564] as follows:

One tenement with a close adjoining to the same	2 a., 3 r., o p.
Of arable land in the fields	6 a., o r., o p.
Common of pasture for 30 sheep upon the down and heath aforesaid	30

Rent 3*s.*, fine [blank], heriot 1
William Talbott and Richard Talbott do hold successively of the grant of Francis Browne esquire and Lady Anne, his wife, by copy dated 15 June year 6th Queen Elizabeth [1564] as follows:

One tenement with orchard and garden and three closes	8a., 0 r., 0 p.
Common of pasture for 60 sheep as is aforesaid	60
Of arable land in the fields	12 a., 0 r., 0 p.

Rent 6*s.* 8*d.*, fine [blank], heriot 1

[Folio 28v]

Martin Earle and Vincent Earle do hold successively by copy dated 15 March year 19th Queen Elizabeth [1577] of the demise of Henry Goringe, esquire, as follows:

One tenement with a garden adjoining to the same	0 a., 0 r., 20 p.

Rent 2*s.* 8*d.*, fine [blank], heriot 1

Joan Baker, widow, and Alice Baker her daughter hold of the demise of Francis Browne, esquire, by copy dated 26 October year 5th and 6th Philip and Mary [1558] as follows:

One tenement with three closes of pasture adjoining to the same	4 a., 0 r., 8 p.
One close adjoining to John Pratant	0 a., 1 r., 8 p.
Of arable lands in the field	20 a., 0 r., 0 p.
Common of pasture for a hundred sheep on the down and heath aforesaid	100

Rent 10*s.* 6*d.*, fine £7., heriot 1

John Haywarde holds for term of his life, of the demise of Sir Thomas Arundell, knight, by a copy dated 19 November year 35 of Henry VIII [1543] as follows:

One tenement with a close adjoining to the same	1 a., 0 r., 0 p.
Of arable land in the common fields	7 a., 0 r., 0 p.
Common of pasture for 40 sheep as is above said	40

Rent 4*s.* 4*d.*, fine 20*s.*, heriot 1

Also one close of pasture at Salterne	1 a., 1 r., 0 p.

Rent 16*d.*

Robert Wotton and John Greene hold there successively of the demise of Henry Goringe, esquire, by a copy dated 6 September year 2nd Queen Elizabeth [1560] as follows:

Four closes and one other close called Sterhayes containing	4 a., 3 r., 0 p.
A tenement newly erected in the same	

Rent 2*s.* fine 20*s.* heriot 1

William Talbott and John Talbott hold of the demise of Margaret Russell, late Abbess of Tarent, by copy dated 2 May year 28th Henry VIII [1537] as follows:

One close of pasture called Brandes containing	15 a., 0 r., 0 p.

Rent 5*s.* 8*d.*, fine [blank], heriot [blank]

[Folio 28v]

Francis Hawley, esquire, holds at the will of the Lord in manner and form following (sometime Henry Bonvile's, before Elizabeth Cradler):

One tenement with certain closes of meadow and pasture adjoining to the same	14 a. 0 r., 0 p.
Of arable land in the fields	39 a., 2 r., 0 p.
Common of pasture for 2 hundred sheep as is above said	200

Rent 20s. fine [blank], heriot [blank]

John Prattant holds to himself, Henry Shattocke and John Prattant, son of the said John, of the demise of John Dodington, steward there, by copy dated 29 May year 25th Elizabeth [1583] as follows:

One toft called Pipershaye	1 a., 0 r., 0 p.

Rent 2s. fine £10

Robert Greene holds for term of his life , of the grant of Sir John de la Lyne, knight, by copy dated 14 August years 2nd and 3rd Philip and Mary [1555] as follows:

One close called Mugghayes	8 a., 0 r., 0 p.
A tenement with a yard	1 a., 1 r., 0 p.
One close called Barkers corner	1 a., 3 r., 9 p.
One close lying at Saltern	5 a., 3 r., 0 p.
Of arable land in the fields	38 a., 0 r., 0 p.
Common of pasture for 2 hundred sheep as is above said	200

Rent 23s., fine £16 13s. 4d., heriot 1

Peter Lawrence, Gertrude his wife and Joan their daughter hold successively for term of their lives, of the demise of John Dodington, steward there, by copy dated 29 October year 25th Elizabeth [1583] one piece of ground as follows:

One piece of waste ground lying at Mogge Wall containing	0 a., 1 r., 0 p.

Rent 12d., fine 20s

Sum: £8 11d.

Alice Nightingall and Alice Cressy hold during their lives one cottage within	0 a., 1 r., 0 p.

Rent 12d. fine 10s. heriot: double the rent

Richard Broun and Thomasine, his wife, hold one cottage during their lives near George Edwards one cottage	0 a., 1 r., 0 p.

Rent 2s., Fine 13s. 4d., heriot: double the rent

[Folio 29r]

Tenants by Indenture

Elizabeth, wife of Richard Squibb, Stephen and William Squibb their sons hold for term of their lives, of the demise of Francis Browne, esquire, and Lady Anne de la Lynde, his wife, by indenture dated 4 January year 1 of Queen Elizabeth [1559] as follows:

The capital mansion house of the demesnes of the said manor	1 a., 0 r., 18 p.
One close over against the same	1 a., 2 r., 36 p.
One meadow called Farme meadow (north 30 yards)	9 a., 2 r., 35 p.
One close against the same	4 a., 1 r., 26p.
Of arable land in the field	180 a., 0 r., 0 p
[Total]	195 a., 3.r., 35 p.
Common of pasture for 5 hundred sheep as is above said	500

Rent £3 8s. 4d., fine £50, worth £30 yearly

They hold more by the same copy lease a coppice called Studland Copice and Castell Leyes, wherein all the customary tenants claim common of estovers, containing	75 a. 0 r., 0 p.
The pasture for sheep on the down contains	173 a., 0 r., 0p.
The waste ground in the heath contains	1210 a., 0 r., 0 p.
The content of all the grounds within this manor is	2015 a., 0 r., 1 p.

A brief note of the whole manor, whereof	
Of pasture in several	128 a., 1 r., 38 p.
Of arable land in the fields	419 a., 2 r., 0 p.
Of meadow	9 a., 2 r., 31 p.
Of coppice woods	46 a., 0r., 0 p.
Sheep pasture upon the downs	173 a., 0 r., 0 p.
Of waste ground in the heath	1210 a., 0 r., 0 p.

Sum of the whole rent of this manor is £11 9s. 3d.

[Folio 35r]

A survey of the manor or lordship of Langton Wallis in the Isle of Purbecke in the Countie of Dorssett, surveyed and measured after 15 foot, 9 inches to the pole or perch in the year of Our Lord 1586

Freeholders

Henry Uevdale, esquire, holds freely to him and his heirs one messuage and certain lands called Sherforde lying near Sherforde bridge, late John Sandford's and before one Hooper's, by suit of court and what other service they know not, and pays yearly for his rent at Michaelmas 4s.

John Clavell, esquire, holds freely to him and his heirs certain lands in Orcharde, late purchased of Simon Davye and before one William Paynes, by suit of court and what other service they know not and pays yearly for his chief rent at the feast aforesaid   6d.

William Culliforde, gentleman, hold freely to him and his heirs certain lands in Quarre, late purchased of William Daccombe, gentleman, by suit of court and what other service they know not and pays yearly for his chief rent at the feast aforesaid   1 d.

Nicholas Percey, gentleman, holds freely to him and his heirs certain lands in Durneforde by suit of court and what other service they know not and pays yearly for his chief rent at the feast aforesaid.

1 d.

Walter Newborough, gentleman, holds freely to him and his heirs certain lands in Easte Orcharde by suit of court and what other service they know not and pays yearly for his chief rent at the feast aforesaid

½ d.

Robert Parmitter holds to him and his heirs certain lands in Burshowe, late parcel of the manor of Alfrington, by suit of court and what other service they know not and pays yearly for his chief rent at the feast aforesaid   ½ d.

William Franke of East Critche holds freely to him and his heirs certain lands in East Critche by suit of court and what other service they know not   Suit of court

Henry Uvedale, esquire, holds freely to him and his heirs certain lands in Newemylles, sometimes John Trewes, by suit of court and what other service they know not   Suit of court

[Folio 35v]

Nicholas Wadham and George Tanner, esquire, hold freely to them and their heirs, certain lands in Bremescombe, sometimes Tregarters, by suit of court and what other services they know not

Suit of court

John Gyll, gentleman, holds freely to him and his heirs certain lands in Langtone Matervers by suit of court and what other service they know not   Suit of court

Sum of the free tenants 4 s. 9 d.

Customary tenants

Agnes Thressher, widow, late wife of George Thressher deceased, holds during her widowhood according to the custom of the manor, of the demise of Anne Willoughby, one tenement which contains as follows:

Item, a tenement and a small meadow adjoining to the same	0 a., 2 r., 25 p.
Item, one close of arable against the same	3 a., 0 r., 33 p.
Item, two closes of pasture called Woode Close	5 a., 2 r., 23 p.
Item, one close of arable among the grounds near the seaside	4 a., 2 r., 31 p.
Item, a close of pasture divided in 2 closes adjoining to the lynche called Heathe Feelde	6 a., 0 r., 39 p.
[Total]	20 a., 0 r., 31 p.

The same Agnes Thressher pays for her yearly rent 5 s. and for a parcel of the demesnes held at will 2 d. And for custom works 4 d. The fine paid at the taking of this farm 13 s. 4 d. No heriot. Heriot none, fine 13 s 4 d.

The reversion of the premises is granted to John Coxe , Cecily Coxe the daughter of Peter Coxe and Alice Charitie the daughter of William Charitie, in the name of one cottage with appurtenances now in the tenure of Agnes Thressher, widow, during her widowhood, is by a copy subscribed by Sir Francis Willoughby, knight, and William Growe dated 24 September 16th year of Queen Elizabeth [1574], one tenement with the lands, by the rents and services as above.
Fine £20

John Browne of the age of 68 years holds for his own life these parcels following:

Item, the house with wood close and the grounds adjoining to the same	6 a., 3 r., 39 p.
Item, 2 furze closes of pasture joining one Culiver's ground	12 a.,1 r.,1 p.
Item, 2 closes of pasture near Norlege Gate	8 a., 1 r., 1 p.
Item, 4 closes of arable against his house	17 a., 2 r., 0 p.
Item, 2 closes of pasture at Stepe Stile	9 a., 1 r., 34 p.
Item a close of arable near the sea side	1 a., 1 r., 38 p.
[Total]	56 a., 0 r., 16 p.

Fine £36

The same John Browne pays for his yearly rent 20s. 10d. and for a parcel of the demesnes held at will 2d. and for customary works 4d. The fine paid for taking his farm £36.
Heriot 1

[Folio 36v]

William Colmann of the age of 57 years holds for his life these parcels following:

Item, the house and two meadows	2 a., 2 r., 36p.
Item, 1 close of pasture by the common	3 a., 1 r., 32 p.
Item, 1 close of pasture against the Langton Farme	11 a., 2 r., 29 p.
Item, a close of pasture by the lynche	9 a., 2 r., 20p.
Item, a close of pasture by the sea side	13 a., 1 r., 36 p.
Item, a close of pasture at Steepe Stile	8 a., 1 r., 6 p.
[Total]	49 a., 1 r., 39 p.

The same William Colmann pays for his yearly rent 18s. and for a parcel of the demesnes held at will 2d. and for customary works 4d. The fine paid at the taking of the farm 26s.
Heriot 1, fine 26s 8d.

Walter Thomse holds to him, to John his son, and Richard Thomse the son of Robert Thomse for term of their lives successively by a copy sealed and subscribed by the said William Grove, steward, dated 23rd September year 16th Queen Elizabeth [1574] which contains:

Item, the house with the ground adjoining to the same	3 a., 0 r., 0 p.
Item, 2 closes of pasture called Heath Feelde	9 a., 2 r., 38 p.
Item, 1 close of pasture called Norlege	7 a., 1 r., 38 p.
Item, 2 closes of arable against his house	11 a., 3 r., 29 p.
Item, 1 close next the sea side	14 a., 0 r., 28 p.
[Total]	46 a., 1 r., 13 p.

The same Walter Thomse pays for his yearly rent 13s. 6d. and for a parcel of the demesnes held at will 2d. and for customary works 4d. The fine paid at the taking of his farm £50

Heriot 1, fine £50.

Richard Trewe holds to him, to Mary and Rebecca for term of their lives successively by a copy of the demise of Sir Francis Williughbye, knight, and subscribed by William Grove, steward, dated 23rd September year 17th Queen Elizabeth [1575] which contains one tenement, viz.:

Item, the tenement with a parcel of meadow	1 a., 3 r., 17 p.
Item, a close of pasture called Wood Close	2 a., 3 r., 9 p.
Item, 2 closes of pasture shouting on Langton Matrevers common[2]	8 a., 1 r., 24 p.
Item, a close against the house, arable	10 a., 0 r., 0 p.
Item, a close of arable among the grounds by the sea side	11 a., 2 r., 9 p.
Item, 2 closes of meadow adjoining to Langton Matreveres common	3 a., 0 r., 1 p.
Item, one other great close of pasture	11 a., 2 r., 22 p.
[Total]	49 a., 1 r., 3 p.

[Folio 37r]

The same Richard Trewe pays for his yearly rent 15s. 8d. and for a parcel of the demesne held at will ~~for~~ 2d. and for customary works 4d. The fine paid at the taking of his farm 40s.

Heriot 1, fine 40s.

George Everye holds to him, to Richard his son and Elizabeth his daughter for term of their lives successively of the demise of the Lady Anne Willoughby, widow, by a copy sealed with the seal and subscribed by Sir Francis Willoughby, knight, Henry Willoughby, esquire, Robert Pemruddocke, steward, and Richard Taverner, receiver, dated 21st March year 32nd of King Henry VIII [1541] one cottage which contains:

Item, the house and croft	0 a., 2 r., 10 p.
Item, one close of arable shouting on Langton Common and Brode Downe	3 a., 0 r., 24 p.
Item, one close of pasture shouting on Walter Thomas heath field	7 a., 1 r., 16 p.
Item, 2 closes of pasture called Norledes	10 a., 3 r., 16 p.
Item, a close adjoining to Bereslade	1 a., 3 r., 0 p.
[Total]	23 a., 2 r., 26 p.

The same George Everye pays for his yearly rent 11s. and for a parcel of the demesnes held at will 2d. and for customary works 4d. the fine paid at the taking of his farm 20s.

Heriot nil, fine 20s.

John Howe of the age of 45 years holds to himself during his life as follows:

Item, the tenement with a croft	0 a., 2 r., 4 p.
Item, a close by the same	1 a., 2 r., 0 p.
Item, a close against the house	0 a., 1 r., 30 p.
Item, a close of pasture shouting on Langton Matrevers common	10 a., 0 r., 10 p.

---

2 "Shouting on" appears to be a Dorset dilect term for one piece of land abutting onto another. It is also used by the surveyor Richard Wright at Durweston, Lytchett Matravers and Okeford Fitzpaine.

Item, one close of arable adjoining to Langton common	2 a., 0 r., 32 p.
Item, one close adjoining to Berslade	13 a., 0 r., 0 p.
Item, a close of arable against the pound	9 a., 2 r., 0 p.
[Total]	37 a., 0 r., 36 p

The same John Howe pays for his yearly rent 11*s*. 8*d*. for a parcel of the demesnes held at will 2*d*. and for customary works 4*d*. the fine paid at the taking of his farm £25.
Heriot 1, fine £25

Richard Cull holds for term of his life as follows:

[Folio 37v]

Item, the house with a parcel of meadow	1 a., 2 r., 0 p.
Item, one other close by the same	1 a., 1 r., 0 p.
Item, one close of arable shouting on Berslad	7 a., 2 r., 25 p.
Item, one close of arable shouting on Langton common	3 a., 0 r., 14 p.
Item, one close of pasture called Heath Feelde	9 a., 0 r., 0 p.
Item, one close of pasture shouting on Matrevers common	10 a., 1 r., 32 p.
Item, a close of arable next the sea side	1 a., 1 r., 38 p.
Item, one other close of arable lying between Houwe and Trew	10 a., 1.r., 3 p.
[Total]	44 a., 3 r., 19 p.

The same Richard Cull pays for his yearly rents 23*s*. 9*d*. and for a parcel of demesnes 2*d*. The fine paid at the taking of the farm 40*s*.
Heriot 1, fine 40*s*.

Richard Edberie holds for term of his life as follows:

Item, the house and 2 closes of pasture	3 a., 1 r., 20 p.
Item, 2 closes of pasture adjoining one Worth common and Langton common	4 a., 0 r., 15 p.
Item, one close against the house	6 a., 3 r., 0 p.
Item, one close near the sea side	15 a., 1 r., 25 p.
Item, one close of pasture shouting on Culls heath field	6 a., 1 r., 12 p.
	35 a., 3 r., 32 p.

The same Richard Edburie pays for his yearly rent 12*s*. and for a parcel of the demesnes held at will 2*d*. And for customary works 4*d*. The fine paid at the taking of the farm £6 13*s*. 4*d*.
Heriot 1, fine £6 13*s*. 4*d*.

George Nightingall holds during his life as follows:

Item, the house with garden, orchard and the great meadow adjoining to the same	7 a., 2 r., 20 p.
Item, the west meadow	4 a., 0 r., 6 p.
Item, the meadow called Well Close	2 a., 2 r., 6 p.
Item, a close of pasture called Whete Close	7 a., 1 r., 13 p.
Item, a close of arable called North Close	3 a.., 3 r., 36 p.
Item, a close of pasture called Deere Feelde	2 a., 2 r., 0 p.

Item a pasture called the Copice	13 a., 2 r., 18 p.
Item, one pasture called East Close with the outer ground and meadows	63 a., 1 r., 33 p.
Item, 3 closes of arable called Eastecombe, Westcombe and Midlecombe	14 a., 2 r., 10 p.
Item, one close of pasture called Norledes	10 a., 0 r., 0 p.
	129 a., 2 r. 22 p.

The same George Nightingall pays for his yearly rent 19s. 6d. The fine paid at the taking of the farm £30 6s. 8d.

Heriots 3, fine £30 6s. 8d.

[Folio 38r]

Agnes Redhed, late the wife of Thomas Redhede deceased, holds during her widowhood according to the custom of the manor, the remainder thereof to John Redhede and George Redheade sons of the said Thomas for term of their lives successively by a copy subscribed by Sir Francis Willoughby, knight, Robert Penruddocke and Richard Mercer, surveyors and steward of the manor, one tenement in Aylewoode called Wester Bargaine dated 27th September year 2nd King Edward VI [1548] which contains as follows:

Item, a tenement called the Wester Bargaine and a close	1 a., 3 r., 28 p.
Item, a close of arable against the same	1 a., 2 r., 0 p.
Item, a close called Wester Hill	4 a., 3 r., 22 p.
Item, a close called West Hey Feelde	3 a., 3 r., 9 p.
Item, one close of pasture called Wester Dunsley	13 a., 3 r., 13 p.
Item, a meadow called Brode Meade	1 a., 1 r., 25 p.
Item, one close called West Hill	3 a., 2 r., 16 p.
Item, one close of pasture called Fursie Hills	3 a., 2 r., 1 p.
Item, one close of arable shouting on Aylywood Doune	2 a., 2 r., 35 p.
	37 a., 0 r., 35 p.

The same Agnes Redhede pays for her yearly rent 10s. 2d. and for customary works 4d. the fine paid at the taking of the farm £20 6s. 8d.

Heriot 1, fine 26s.

Common for 50 sheep on Aylywood Downe

The said Agnes holds during her widowhood one other tenement in Aylywoode called the Easter Bargaine, the remainder thereof to Richard Redhead and William Redhed two other of the sons of the said Thomas for term of their lives successively by a copy subscribed by the said Sir Francis Willoughby, knight, and William Grove dated 24th September year 15th Queen Elizabeth [1573] which contains as follows:

Item, the tenement with garden and orchard	0- a., 2 r., 20 p.
Item, one close of arable by the same	10 a., 2 r., 6 p.
Item, a meadow called the Little Meade	3 a., 0 r., 6 p.
Item, 2 closes of pasture East Hill	9 a., 0 r., 34 p.
Item, a parcel of meadow in the same	1 a., 1 r.., 0 p.
Item, one close of pasture divided into 2 closes called Dunsley	7 a., 3 r., 36 p.
Item, one close of pasture called Watt Hill	2 a., 2 r., 29 p.
Item, a parcel of meadow called Watt Hill Mead	1 a., 0 r., 5 p.
	36 a., 1 r., 16 p.

[Folio 38v]

The same Agnes Redhed pays for her yearly rent 10s. 4d. and for customary works 4d. fine paid at the taking of the farm £20.
Heriot 1, fine £20.

Common for 50 sheep on Aliwood Downe

Robert Gentle holds to him, to Julian Urraye and Alice Urraye daughters of Robert Urraye for term of their lives successively by a copy sealed and subscribed by Sir Francis Willoughbie, knight, and subscribed by William Grove, dated Wednesday the sixth of April year 11th Queen Elizabeth [1569] one tenement which contains as follows:

Item, the tenement with orchard and garden	0 a., 2 r., 16 p.
Item, one close of arable near the same	2 a., 0 r., 10 p.
Item, a meadow by the same	3 a., 2 r., 0 p.
Item, one close of arable called Easter Feelde	9 a., 0 r., 8 p.
Item, one meadow called Woot Hill Meade	0 a., 3 r., 10 p.
Item, one close of pasture called Woot Hill	5 a., 3 r., 16 p.
Item, 2 closes called Newe Close and Whete Close	7 a., 3 r., 8 p.
Item, a meadow called Rise Meade	1 a., 0 r., 2 p.
Item, one close of arable called Rise Hill	3 a., 2 r., 34 p.
Item, one close of pasture called Over Heath Feelde	4 a., 3 r., 10 p.
Item, Nether Heath Feeld with 2 parcels of meadow	12 a., 2 r., 24 p.
Item, a close of arable called Methhaye	0 a., 3 r., 6 p.
	52 a., 2 r., 24 p.
The same Robert Gentle pays for his yearly rent	13s. 4d.
Fine paid at the taking of the farm	£66 13s. 4d.

Heriot 1, fine £66 13s. 4d.

Common for 80 sheep on Aliwood Downe

William Grove the younger holds to him, to Margaret Grove the daughter of William Grove, brother of the said William Grove the younger, and Anne the daughter of David Grove, another brother of the said William for term of their lives successively, by a copy sealed and subscribed by the said Sir Francis Willoughbye, knight, etc. subscribed by William Grove, steward, dated Thursday the eleventh of October year 13th Queen Elizabeth [1571] one tenement which contains as follows:

[Folio 39r]

Item, the tenement with garden	0 a., 1 r., 14 p.
Item, the meadow against the same	0 a., 3 r., 30 p.
Item, a close of pasture called Woott Close	5 a., 0 r., 10 p.
Item, a close of pasture called Drye Close	4 a., 2 r., 0 p.
Item, the meadow by the same	3 a., 2 r., 0 p.
Item, a pasture called Dursley	3 a., 2 r., 14 p.
Item, a rushy meadow beneath the same	3 a., 1 r., 39 p.
Item, one close of arable called Ote Hill	5 a., 1 r., 3 p.
Item, one close of arable called Ester Feelde	9 a., 2 r., 0 p.

Item, one close of pasture called Anstons Hill | 7 a., 3 r., 30 p.

44 a., 0 r., 20 p.

The same William Growe pays for his yearly rent 12s.
Heriot 1, fine £36.
Common of pasture for 70 sheep on Aylywood Downe

Sum of the acres in the tenures of the customary tenants | 672 a., 3 r., 26 p.

Sum total of the rents of customary tenants £10 19d.

The customary tenants hold adjoining to the woods a common of pasture
being a very bushy ground called Lynches alias Langton Common which
contains by measure | 25 a., 0 r., 0p.

The customary tenants hold there a sheep walk which extends from
Kingdowne into Alliwood grounds and contains by measure | 77 a., 1 r., 22 p.

There is within this manor one wood called Langtonn Woode which
contains by measure | 40 a., 0 r., 0 p.

Also one other coppice called the Easte Coppice which contains by
measure | 30 a., 0 r., 0 p.

[Folio 39v]

Tenants by indenture:

William Grove holds by indenture dated [blank] of [blank] all the cottage and farm house of Langtonn
Wallis late in the occupation of John Samways, gentleman, containing these parcels following:

Item, the farm house with a meadow called Meathaye	3 a., 0 r., 27 p.
Item, one close, sometime 2 closes, called Wood Close	10 a., 1 r., 0 p.
Item, one pasture called Litle Downe	20 a., 1 r., 4 p.
Item, a meadow called Hethersey	5 a., 2 r., 10 p.
Item, a great pasture called West Feeld and Broade Downe	218 a., 3 r., 35 p.
Item, a pasture called the Wallis	11 a., 1 r., 24 p.
Item, a close of arable next the same	12 a., 1 r., 2 p.
Item, a close of pasture called Highe Landes being part of West Field	67 a., 2 r., 39 p.
Item, a meadow called Abrehaye	1 a., 3 r., 8 p.
Item, a meadow in Sandwich by the bridge called Ingrames Meade	2 a., 0 r., 0 p.
Item, the winter pasture of a meadow in Sandwiche	1 a., 2 r., 0 p.
Item, one pasture sometime 4 closes called Greate Thorne Little Thorne, Sawlese Close and Fowkwath	96 a., 1 r .,3 p.
Item, a close of pasture called Bearslade	12 a., 1 r., 24 p.
The same William Grove pays for his yearly rent £66 13s. 4d.	
	463 a., 3 r., 10 p.

Item, the said William Grove has also common of pasture with his rother beasts according to his tenure in the wood called Langtonn Woode

John Havellande, gentleman, holds by indenture to him and Thomas his son for term of their lives the farm called Wilkeswoode also Wilchwoode

Item, the house with garden, orchard and meadow by the same	6 a., 0 r., 0 p.
Item, the Lynches being pasture and meadow with the ponds	16 a., 3 r., 17 p.
Item, 2 closes of pasture and meadow of the demesnes lying on the back of the parsonage	15 a., 1 r., 19 p.
Item, 2 closes of pasture called Norleades	9 a., 2 r., 18 p.
Item, a meadow next Mr Paye's house	1 a., 1 r., 8 p.
Item, 3 closes of arable called Proyers	9 a., 0 r., 0 p.
Item, 1 close of arable and 2 of pasture adjoining to Mr Percye his ground	73 a., 2 r., 15 p.
Item, a parcel of ground in Haycrofte with a cottage	0 a., 2 r., 0 p.
Item, a parcel of ground with a cottage called Lytle Byndon	0 a., 0 r., 16 p.
Item, a close of arable and pasture called Wester Norles and Easter Norleys	7 a., 2 r., 28 p.
Item, 3 pastures called Barnswoode	56 a., 2 r., 4 p.
Item, in Worth Feelde	29 a., 0 r., 2 p.
Item, East Langton Felde	14 a., 0 r., 0 p.
Item, a meadow at the east end of Lynches	2 a., 2 r., 0 p.
	247 a., 0 r., 7 p.

[Folio 40r]

The same John Havellaunde pays for his yearly rent £5 12d.
The fine paid at the taking of the farm £100.

The same John Havellande holds by lease for 21 years Dated the 6 of July in the 26 year of her Majesty's reign, a pasture called the West Copice containing	23 a., 2 r., 6 p.

The same John Havellande pays for his yearly rent 20s.
The fine paid at the taking of the farm £50.

Henry Uvedale, esquire, Edmond Uvedall and John Uvedale his sons hold for the term of their lives by indenture the pasture called Newe Milles as follows:

Item, 3 closes of pasture	16 a., 1 r., 39 p.
Item, of meadow the moiety of two plots	0 a., 1 r., 26 p.
	16a., 3 r., 25 p.

The same Henry Uvedall, esquire, pays for his yearly rent 12s.

Eleanor late wife of John Bridges and William Briges her son holds for term of their lives by indenture the farm with the grounds called Midleburey:

Item, the house with orchard and garden	0 a., 3 r., 0 p.
Item, a close called Pease Close, arable	4 a., 3 r., 18 p.

Item, the home ground whereof part is arable	25 a., 3 r., 21 p.
Item, a close called Rie Close, the one half arable, the other pasture	5 a., 1 r., 1 p.
Item, the great pasture ground being furze	98 a., 3 r., 33 p.
Item, a close by the same, of arable	1 a., 0 r., 20 p.
Item, a pasture by the Orde	15 a., 1 r., 38 p.
Item, one other pasture called the Orde with the Saltes	24 a., 0 r., 2 p.
	177 a., 1 r., 13 p.

There is also belonging to this farm a heath called Middelbery
Heath and Langtonn Heath which contains   885 a., 0 r., 20 p.
and in the name of a heriot 40s.

The same Eleanor pays for her yearly rent 40s. The fine paid at the taking of the farm £80.

[Folio 40v]

The same heath aforesaid belonging to the manor of Langton and farm of Midelberye is bounded and follows from Mydleburye House to Flokes Forde from Flokes Forde to Neither Crosse Water, from Neither Crose Water to Overcrose Water, from Overcrose Water to Herstone, from Herstone to A Hiphill of Stones from thence to Hickslyde Bridge, from thence to Hichslade Head, from thence to Kype Crosse, from thence one furlong [blank] unto two thorns, from thence to Horethorne, from thence to Wythy Lake and then kept the lake to Sharfoorde Bridge, which contains in all by measure as aforesaid.

William Dyet holds for term of his life by indenture dated the 20th day of March 32nd of the reign of King Henry VIII [1541] by the grant of Dame Anne Willoughbye of Woodlande in the county of Dorsett.

Item, one parcel of meadow lying and being in Rushton Meade in the parish of Stoke	14 a., 0 r., 0 p.

The same William Dyet pays for his yearly rent 13s. 4d.
The fine paid at the taking of the farm £4 10d.

Sum of acres of this manor	2673 a., 2 r., 9 p.

Sum total of the tenants by indenture, £75 19s. 8d.

The whole rent of the manor of Langton Wallis, £86 6s.

The custom of the manor of Langton Wallys by the oaths of the tenants:

Firstly, where but one life is in possession the Lord may grant three lives in reversion. Also that the wife of every customary tenant dying possessed of any customary tenement shall have her widow's estate in the same and that every customary tenant except the cottagers and widows shall pay a heriot at his death.

Also that every tenant may make a quarry for tile stone in his ground, paying to the lord for every load thereof one penny.

And that the lord may keep as well a leet as a court baron upon the manor and that the liberties incident to the same leet extend over all the grounds appertaining to the manor and that all waifs, strays, treasure trove, goods and chattels of felons and fugitives are incident to the lord of the same manor.

And that the purchaser may surrender the reversioner's estate so that the reversioners do pay no part of the fine.

And that the tenants of Langton Wallis have always dug turves in Langton Heath adjoining unto Midelbery Heath, which common is bounded by a way to the north side of the gallows from the port way east unto Thorne moor.

[Folio 43r]

The survey of the manor of Eastington in the Isle of Purbecke, in the county of Dorset, the plot whereof is set forth in the plot of Langton Wallis and measured at 15 foot 9 inches to the perch in the year of Our Lord 1586.

Freeholders

William Chalcott, gentleman, holds freely to him and to his heirs certain lands and tenements in East Kimeredge called Chalcotts Landes by knight's service and pays   16s.

William Cyferwast, gentleman, holds freely to him in the right of his wife, late wife to Thomas Dackombe, gentleman, certain lands in Quarr and in other places near Corfe by knight's service and pays
16d.

Hugh Cheverell, esquire, holds freely to him and his heirs certain lands and tenements called Kimeridge, late Thomas Arney's, by knight's service and pays yearly   3s. 4d.

John Clavell, esquire, holds freely certain lands in Little Kimridge by knight's service and pays yearly
20d.

The same John Clavell holds freely to him and to his heirs certain lands called Smedmore by knight's service and pays yearly   8s.

The same John Clavell holds of Alfrington freely of Our Sovereign Lady the Queen by knight's service and pays yearly   2s.

The same John Clavell holds certain lands and tenements in Langton, late George Gerrord, gentleman, and late Robert Rawlines, by knight's service and pays yearly 13s. 4d. and pays at his death in the name of five heriots 20s. and for relief 13s. 4d. and pays yearly   13s. 4d.

John Sandeforde holds one close near Corf Castell called Rye Croft by knight's service and pays yearly
1 lb of cumin.

[Folio 43v]

Thomas Gouer holds freely certain lands lying in the east part of Ungarson called Tappats Hayes late Robert Hardy's and before the Lord Bonvil's   2s.

Sum of the freeholders is 47s. 8d. and 1 lb of cumin.

The manor house of Estington with the demesnes

William Grove holds by indenture the manor house

With the pasture called Southe Feelde	42 a., 3 r., 26 p.
The pasture called Midle Feelde	62 a., 1 r., 10 p.
The feelde of arable called Minbarowe	35 a., 1 r., 30 p.
The meadow called Rowe Meddow and	
The meadow called Minbarowe Meadow	32 a., 0 r., 16 p.
The pasture called South Feeld alias Moles Downe	142 a., 2 r., 31 p.
The parcel of ground called Parke Meadowe	5 a., 2 r., 12 p.
The parcel of meadow called Wythie Beade	1 a., 3 r., 17 p.
The parcel of ground called the Orcharde Meade	2 a., 2 r., 30 p.

325a., 2 r., 12 p.

The same William Grove pays yearly for rent £66 13s. 4d.

Francis Hawley, esquire, holds at will certain lands, meadow and pasture belonging to the same manor called Heycrofts.

Item, Upper Haycroftes with a cottage in it being pasture	11 a., 0 r., 27½ p.
Item, a small close of pasture near the same	2 a., 2 r., 32 p.
Item, the pasture called Nether Haycroftes	18 a., 2 r., 12 p.
Item, a parcel of meadow	2 a., 1 r., 18 p.
	34 a., 3 r., 2½ p.

The same Francis Hawley pays for his yearly rent £5

Sum total of the rent of Eastington £74 12d.

[Folio 45v]

The survey of the manor of Alfrington alias Aldrington in the Isle of Purbucke, in the county of Dorsett, with the grounds belonging to the same.

Freeholders:

William Daccombe, gentleman, holds freely certain lands in Burshewe and the mill called Afflett Myll and pays yearly	15s.
John Clavell, esquire, holds freely certain lands in Orcharde and pays yearly therefore	7s.
Henry Bonvile holds freely certain lands in the manor of Alfrington and pays yearly	½ lb of pepper
George Uvedall, gentleman, holds freely in the right of his wife certain lands in Wulgerston and pays yearly	3s.

Jerrard Attye holds freely certain lands in Alfrington and pays yearly ... 8*d.*

John Sewarde holds freely certain lands in Wulgarston and pays yearly ... 16*d.*

William Daccombe holds freely certain lands in Wulgarstonn and pays yearly ... 5*d.*

Allyn Frampton holds freely certain lands in Pimphorne called Hedley and pays yearly ... 5*s.*

John Wadhame, esquire, holds freely certain lands in Wulgerston and pays 16*d.*

      Sum 35*s.* 1*d.* and half a pound of pepper

[Folio 46r]

Francis Hawley, esquire, holds at will the moiety of the site of the manor and the moiety of all the demesnes sometime in the tenure of Robert Dollinge the elder and also the sixth part of the same site and demesne lands as follows:

Item, the site of the house with orchard and pounds	2 a., 0 r., 33 p.
Item, one half of a pasture called Heath Feelde	17 a., 3 r., 37 p.
Item, a pasture called Easte Heath Feelde	22 a., 1 r., 4 p.
Item, a pasture called Haycroftes	26 a., 2 r., 24 p.
Item, a pasture called New Leeyes	15 a., 1 r., 6 p.
Item, a meadow called Gauskones	1 a., 3 r., 8 p.
Item, a meadow which has been divided into many parcels called Eastmeade	10 a., 0 r., 0 p.
Item, a parcel of meadow adjoining to Skoles	1 a., 1 r., 0 p.
Item, a close called Skulles Close	2 a., 3 r., 10 p.
Item, a pasture called Tumberlands	4 a., 1 r., 20p.
Item, a pasture called Buttesbrough	14 a., 0 r., 28 p.
Item, a pasture called Crofts	5 a., 0 r., 35 p.
Item, a pasture called West Feelde	5 a., 2 r., 20 p.
Item, a field of arable called North-East Feelde	43 a., 0 r., 15 p.
Item, a field called North-West Feelde	53 a., 3 r., 34 p.
Item, a parcel of arable called Sheepehayes	7 a., 2 r., 32 p.
Item, a one other field adjoining to Worth	45 a., 1 r., 18 p.
Item, a part of a mead called West Mead	4.a., 3 r., 8 p.
Item, a parcel of wood ground called Affrington Grove	5 a., 0 r., 0 p.
Item, a parcel of meadow whereon stands a tenement decayed	2 a., 3 r., 36 p.
	292 a., 2 r., 8 p.

The same Francis Hawly pays for the moiety of the site of the manor and the moiety of all the demesnes ... £33 6*s.* 8*d.*

The same Francis Hawly for the sixth part of the site and demesnes keeps a plough for the necessary service at the castle of the lord from time to time.

[Folio 46v]

Robert Dollinge of Corfe holds during the lives of his father and himself, by the grant of Robert Hardie some time lord of the same manor, these parcels following:

Item, a meadow called Cowe Close meadow	2 a., o r., 10 p.
Item, a close of pasture called Cowe Close [margin] in Dacome	7 a., o r., 29 p.
Item, one other small meadow called Cowe Close meadow	2 a., o r., 10 p.
	11 a., 1 r., 19 p.

Elizabeth Hobbes late wife of Robert Hardie holds for term of her life this parcel following:

Item, a close of pasture called Great Dypshels	7 a., o r., o p.
Item, a part of a meadow called West Meade	3 a., 3 r., 30 p.
Item, another close of pasture called Little Dipshels	3 a., 1 r., 36 p.
Item, the moiety or one half of Heath Feelde	17 a., 3 r., 37 p.
Item, a close called West Feelde	5 a., 2 r., 17 p.
Item, one close adjoining to Kingston	33 a., 3 r., 3 p.
	71 a., 3 r., 3 p.

Sum of the whole rent of this manor is: £35 21d. and ½ lb of pepper.

[Folio 47r]

A brief note of whole rents of the manor and lands aforesaid:

The rents and revenues of the Castle of Corfe is	£20 8s. 7d.,	2 lb of wax
		1 lb of cumin
		1 lb of pepper
		35 bsh of wheat
The rent of the manor of Studland is	£11 9s. 4d.	
The rent of the manor of Langton Wallys is	£86 6s.	
The rent of the manor of Estington is	£74 12d.	1 lb of cumin
The rent of the manor of Aflington is	£35 21d.	½ lb of pepper

Sum total of all the rents within the Isle of Purbeck:	£227 6s. 7d.
Whereof to be paid at Our Lady Day	£107 5s. 8d.
And at Michaelmas	£120 11d.
The rents of the lands at Wareham without the Isle is	£10 16s.
The fee of the Bailiwick of Waymouth, Wyke, Hallwell, Portland and Wareham, together with the hundreds of Rambarowe, Rushmore and Haseller by year	£6.
Sum total of all the rent and revenues, with the fee of the Bailliwick aforesaid is	£244 2s. 7d.

KEY TABLES ACCOMPANYING TRESWELL'S MAPS

A brief rental and survey of all the lands and rents belonging to the Castle of Corfe in the Isle of Purbeck, which are not all set forth in this plot, but in other plots following in this book more at large.

Free Tenants	*Rents*	*Acres, roods and perches*
The free tenants 4 lb wax, 1 lb pepper, 1 lb of cummin and 35 bsh of wheat	28s. 9d.	
Tenants at will		
The bailiff of Corfe for Holwiche meade	8s.	7, 0, 0
The same bailiff for a pasture called Gosseham	3s.	2, 0, 0
John Haward of Newton for a parcel of ground	18d.	
Tenants by Copy		
John Haward for a tenement called Newton	14s.	724, 0, 4
The same for inclosed grounds, arable and pasture		42, [0], 4
The same of heath ground belonging to the same tenement		682, 0, 0
Richard Tupp for a tenement and inclosed grounds	23s. 4d.	35, 3, 24
The same Richard Tupp has common for sheep on Ulwell Downe *saune num'* [without number?]		
Tenants by Deed		
William Newman for the demesnes of the castle and mill	£7 13s. 4d.	124, 2, 12
John Uvedall, gentleman, for a burgage with a curtilage	5s.	0, 2, 0
William Grove for the pasture of 60 sheep on Kingsdown	2s.	36, 2, 36
The bailiff of Corfe for arable land in Westhaws	40s.	8, 0, 0
Henry Durrante for the moiety of Ulwell mill	6s. 8d.	
Thomas Crass for a parcel of ground called the Ham	16d.	0, 0, 30
Chevage money alias Deare Month Silver		
The same for the tithing of diverse lordships and towns		19s.
Fodder hay 4 loads, hens 10, salt 26 bsh, wheat 35 bsh, or		22s. 8d.
The same, rent for lands and gardens at Wareham, with other fees		£20 16s.
The same, one wood called Kinges Wood set forth in Langton plot		39, 2, 36

Elinor late wife of John Bridges and William Bridges her son hold for term of their lives by indenture the farm with the grounds called Middleburey as follows:	*Acres, roods and perches*
The house with orchard and garden and a close of pasture called Pease close	5, 2, 18
One close called the Home ground whereof part is arable and part pasture	25, 3, 21
One close of arable and pasture called Rye close	5, 1, 1
One close of arable by the same	1, 0, 20
The great pasture being full of furseys [furze]	98, 3, 33
One pasture called the Orde now divided into two closes	39, 2, 0
The heath called Myddelbury heath	885, 0, 20
Sum:	1062 a., 1 r., 33 p.
The rent of this farm and grounds is 40s. and in the name of a heriot 40s.	

A survey of the manor or lordship of Langton Wallis in the Isle of Purbeck in the county of Dorset measured 15 foot 9 inches to the perch, Anno Domini 1585

Charac ters	Rents	Dem esnes	Custom works	Her iots	Customary tenants	Acres of meadow	Acres of arable	Acres of pasture
☽	5 s.	2 d.	4 d.	0	Agnes Thrasher holds by copy for her widowhood one tenement	0, 2, 25	7, 3, 24	11, 3, 22
★	20 s. 10 d.	2 d.	4 d.	1	John Browne holds for his life one tenement and	2, 0, 0	18, 3, 38	35, 0, 18
🐦	18 s.	2 d.	4 d.	1	William Colman holds for his life on tenement and	2, 3, 36	19, 0, 0	27, 2, 3
⚘	13 s. 6 d.	2 d.	4 d.	1	Walter Thomse, John Thomse and Richard Thomse hold a tenement	1, 0, 0	26, 0, 17	19, 0, 36
◇	15 s. 8 d.	2 d.	4 d.	1	Richard Trewe, Mary and Rebecca his daughters: a tenement and	4, 3, 18	24, 2, 10	22, 3, 15
⚜	11 s.	2 d.	4 d.	0	George Everey and Richard his son hold one tenement and	0, 2, 10	4, 3, 24	18, 0, 32
♂	11 s.	2 d.	4 d.	1	John Howe holds for his own life one tenement and	1, 2, 0	24, 2, 32	11, 0, 4
O	23 s. 9 d.	2 d.	0	1	Richard Cull holds for his life one tenement and	2, 3, 0	22, 2, 27	19, 1, 32
✿	12 s.	2 d.	4 d.	1	Richard Edburey holds for his life one tenement and	1, 0, 0	22, 0, 25	12, 3, 7
⚕	19 s. 6 d.	0	0	3	George Nyghtingall holds for his life one tenement and	24, 1, 30	21, 1, 25	93, 1, 21
✠	10 s. 2 d.	0	4 d.	1	Agnes Redhed, John and George Redhed: a tenement and	1, 1, 25	4, 0, 35	31, 2, 15
✝	10 s. 4 d.	0	4 d.	1	Agnes Redhed, Richard and William her sons: a tenement and	5, 1, 11	10, 2, 6	20, 1, 39
⚓	13 s. 4 d.	0	-	1	Robert Gentle, Julian and Alice Urray holds one tenement and	6, 2, 0	20, 0, 0	26, 0, 24
✠	12 s.	0	0	1	William Grove, Margaret and Anne Grove hold one tenement and	4, 1, 30	14, 3, 3	24, 3, 27
Sum of rent £10 19 d.						Sum: 672 a., 3 r., 26 p.		
Item: there is belonging to some of these tenants a sheep walk called Aylewood Downe containing 77 a., 1 r., 22 p. in the which four have common for 210 sheep.								

Characters	Rents	Tenants by indenture	Acres of meadow	Acres of arable	Acres of pasture
G	£66 13 s. 4 d.	William Grove a farm called Langton farm	14, 0, 5	30, 0, 0	419, 3, 5
H	£5 12 d.	John Havelland a farm called Wilchwoode	6, 2, 0	126, 2, 15	113, 3, 32
H	20 s.	John Havelland a pasture called West Copice	0, 0, 0	0, 0, 0	23, 2, 6
Sum of rent £72 14 s. 4 d.			Sum 734 a., 1 r., 23 p.		
The tenants hold a common very bushy called Lynches adjoining to the woods containing			25 a., 0 r., 0 p.		
		Woods in Langton Wallis			
Item, one wood called Langton Wood			40 a., 0 r., 0 p.		
Item, one coppice called East Coppice			30 a., 0 r., 0 p.		
12 s.		Henrye Uvedale esquire for Newe Milles	0, 1, 26	0, 0, 0	16, 1, 39
40 s.		Elionor late wife of Bridges for Midleburye	0, 0, 0	20, 0, 0	1042, 1, 37

13s. 4d.	William Diet holds Rushton Meade in Stoke	14, 0, 0	0, 0, 0	0, 0, 0
The rents of freeholders which hold of [the] manor		4s. 9d.		
The contents of all the grounds within this manor		2673 a., 2 r., 27 p.		
The rents of the whole manor of Langton Wallis		£86 6s.		

A survey of the manor of Eastington set forth in this plot and measured as before	
William Grove holds by indenture these parcels following paying yearly	£66 13s. 4d.
Item, the site of the manor with South Feeldes and Nicoles Downe	185, 2, 17
Item, one other pasture called Midlefeeld	62, 1, 10
Item, one field of arable called Nunbarowes	35, 1, 30
Item, one meadow called Rowe meadow	32, 0, 16
Item, three meadows called Parke meadow, Withey Bede and Orchard	10, 0, 19
Sum	325 a., 2 r., 12 p.
Frauncis Hawley esquire holds at will these parcels following, paying yearly	£5
Item, three closes of pasture called Haycroftes	32, 1, 31½
Item, a parcel of meadow	2, 1, 18
Chief rents paid yearly one pound of cumin and 47s. 8d.	
Sum of the rent of this manor £74 12d. and of acres 360 a., 1 r., 21 p.	

The survey of the manor of Studlande in the Isle of Purbecke in the County of Dorset measured at 15 foot 9 inches to the perch						
Characters	The names of the tenants	Arable in the field	Meadow and pasture	Rents	Fine (last)	Heriots
	William Monday holds a tenement	11, 2, 0	5, 0, 0	6s.	£26	1
	John Talbott holds one tenement and	11, 2, 0	8, 0, 0	7s. 1d.	£50	1
	Edith Wilshire holds one tenement and	11, 2, 0	2, 3, 20	6s.	£11	1
	Edith Cotton holds one tenement and	6, 0, 0	2, 0, 4	4s.	-	1
	Thomas Ricards holds one tenement and	11, 0, 0	1, 1, 0	6s. 8d.	30s.	1
	Elionour Colman holds one tenement	6, 0, 0	3, 3, 0	5s.	-	-
	William Mose holds one tenement	8, 0, 0	3, 0, 19	4s. 4d.	£30	1
	Alice Talbot holds one tenement	11, 2, 0	2, 0, 2	6s. 4d.	40s.	1
	Phillipp Forde one tenement and	18, 0, 0	14, 3, 23	16s. 7d.	£80	2
	Joanne Marchaunt one tenement and	26, 0, 0	8, 0, 24	13s. 8d.	-	1
	Joanne Branne one tenement and	6, 0, 0	1, 1, 0	3s.	-	1
	William Strowde holds one tenement	6, 0, 0	2, 3, 0	3s.	-	1
	W. Talbott holds one tenement and	12, 0, 0	8, 0, 0	6s. 8d.	-	1
	Martin Earle one tenement and	0, 0, 0	0, 0, 20	2s. 8d.		1
	Joanne Baker one tenement and	20, 0, 0	4, 1, 16	10s. 6d.	£7	1
	John Hawarde one tenement and	7, 0, 0	2, 1, 0	5s. 8d.	20s.	-
	Robert Wutton one tenement and	4, 0, 0	4, 3, 0	2s.	20s.	1
	Frauncis Hawley one tenement	39, 2, 0	14, 0, 0	20s.	-	-
	John Pratant one tenement and	-	1, 1, 0	2s.	£10	-
	Robert Greene one tenement and	38, 0, 0	17, 1, 9	23s.	£16 13s. 4d.	1
	William Talbott holds Brandes	0, 0, 0	15, 0, 0	5s. 8d.	-	-
	Peter Lawrence one cottage	0, 0, 0	0, 1, 0	12d.	20s.	-
	Elizabeth wife of Richard Squibb	180, 0, 0	16, 3, 35	£3 8s. 4d.	£50	-
	Elizabeth S[quibb] holds Studland Wood	-	75, 0, 0	-	-	-
	The Heathe ground	-	1210, 0, 0	-	-	-

	The Downe or sheep pasture	-	173, 0	-	-	-
	Sum of the pasture and meadow in several	138 a., 0 r., 29 p.				
	Sum of arable land in the fields	419 a., 2 r., 0 p.				
	Manor with Studland Wood, the Downe and Heathe is	2015 a., 2 r., 29 p.				
	Sum of the yearly rent of this manor	£11 9s. 3d.				

John Hawarde holds by copy one tenement with these parcels following	
The house with orchard and withy bed	4 a., 2 r., 8 p.
One close of arable called Southe close	5 a., 0 r., 1 p.
One close Westhaye and Wintershaye	8 a., 0 r., 19 p.
One close called Easthaye	4 a., 3 r., 19 p.
One close called Clewelshey	5 a., 1 r., 8 p.
One other close called Clewelshey	4 a., 3 r., 8 p.
One other close of arable in the same	0 a., 3 r., 33 p.
One close of arable by the same	2 a., 1 r., 0 p.
One close called Shannor Poynte	2 a., 0 r., 18 p.
One close called Dygnelshaye	3 a., 3 r., 0 p.
Newton heath with the Isle called Grove	682 a., 0 r., 0 p.
Sum	724 a., 0 r., 4 p.
The same John Haward pays for his yearly rent	14s.
The fine paid at the taking of this farm	£3 6s. 8d.
Heriot	One

INDEX

This is an index of personal and place names in the introduction and transcription of the written survey.

Spain 15, 34
Squibb, Elizabeth 164
  Richard 164
  Stephen 164
  William 164
Stanton (Cambridgeshire) 4
Strowde, William 161
Studland, Studlande, Stodlond 3, 5, 8, 18–21, 30, 33,
    36–8, 53, 55, 58, 159–64
  Agglestone Rock 36
  Black Down 36
  Castle 20–1, 153
  field names, Barkers 163
    Brandes 162
    Castell Leyes 20–1, 164
    Clewelsheye 150
    Coke 38
    Dingelshaye 150
    East Castle 20
    East Field, East Feelde 19–20
    East Salterne 37, 161
    Easte Haye 150
    Farme Meadowe 160, 164
    Geries 38
    Grove 150
    Mogge Wall 163
    Monthays 161
    Mugghayes 163
    Pipershaye 163
    Rede 38
    Rickmans 38
    Ryecroft 36
    Salterne 21, 159–63
    Shannor Poynte 150
    South Close 150
    South East Castle 20
    Sterhayes 162
    Studland Copice 164
    West Castle 20
    West Salterne 21, 37, 161
    Weste Haye 150
    Winters Haye 150
    Withie Beade 149
  Greenland Farm 22
  Hanfast Point 21, 34, 37–8
  Heath 36
  King Barrow 19, 21
  Little Sea 21–2, 37–8
  Newton 8, 23, 34, 149, 152
  Newton Farm 34
  Newton Bay, alias The Hope 38–39
  Newton Heath 31, 37–9, 150
  Pinnacles, The 37
  South Haven 21–2, 37–8
  St Lucas Leap 21, 37
  Studland Down 19
  Studland Heath 19

  Studland Wood 20–1
  West Field, West Feelde 19–20
Sturmer Mere, (Essex) 39
Sturminster Newton 28
Swanage, Sanwich, Sandwich 28, 55
  field names, Beane Close 150
    Brooke Meadowe 150
    Gille Combe 150
    Gille Haye 150
    Ingrames Meade 171
    Mill Haye 150
    Ridge Acre 150
    Touthills 150
    Ulwell Downe 150
    Whitleyes, Whitleys 150
    Whitly Downe 150
  Ulwell 150–1
  Ulwell, Grist mill 150
Sydling St Nicholas 56

Talbot, Talbott, family 52
  Alice 160
  Anthony 159
  John 159, 162
  Richard 162
  Urie 159
  William 159–60, 162
Tanner, George 165
Tappats Hayes 174
Taverner, Richard 167
Thomse, John 166
  Richard 166
  Robert 166
  Walter 166–7
Thorpe (Northamptonshire) 9
Thorpe, Thomas (cartographer) 40
Thressher, Agnes 165
  George 165
Toddington (Bedfordshire) 29
Tregarter, family 165
Treswell, Ralph, junior (cartographer) 30
  Ralph, senior (cartographer) 1, 4, 7–9, 11, 13–15,
    17–18, 20–3, 25–6, 28–36, 39–41, 45–6, 51–2,
    54, 56–7
Trewe, John 147–8, 165
  Mary 167
  Rebecca 167
  Richard 167
  William 149
Tuppe, Richard 150
Tye, family 52
  John 148
Tyneham, Tynehame, East 33, 55, 152
Tyneham, Tynehame, West 55, 152

Ungarson 174
Urraye, Alice 170

Lightning Source UK Ltd.
Milton Keynes UK
UKOW07n1533301117
313636UK00005B/42/P